THE PRACTI

ELK HUNTING

FORTY YEARS OF ELK HUNTING LESSONS

JOHN A. CLEVELAND

The Practical Guide to Elk Hunting; Forty Years of Elk Hunting Lessons

Published By: Lodgepole Books, Littleton, Colorado
Copyright ©2019 John A. Cleveland. All Rights Reserved

ISBN: 978-0-578-51160-3
Sports & Recreation/Hunting

Illustrations by Jordyn Callandret
Front cover and back cover photos by Frances F. Cleveland
Cover and Interior design by Victoria Wolf

QUANTITY PURCHASES: Schools, companies, professional groups, clubs and other organizations may qualify for special terms when ordering quantities of this title. For information, E-Mail jaclevelandcolo@gmail.com

DEDICATION

*I dedicate this book to my grandfather, Thomas D'Arcy Brophy.
If not for his spirit, I would not be here today.*
*I also dedicate this book to my wife, Frances, whose steadfast
advocacy saved my right leg.*

TABLE OF CONTENTS

INTRODUCTION

This book is written primarily to help the first time, or early time, "do-it-yourself" type elk hunter. By "do-it-yourself" I mean the person who goes out by him/herself, or perhaps with a group of friends, and hunts, boots on the ground, for elk.

I also think this book will benefit more experienced hunters interested in improving their skills and increasing their hunting success. While I hunt with a rifle, I think that many of the lessons I have learned are also applicable to a bow hunter. As well, I think hunters who use guide services will benefit by making them more knowledgeable about elk and elk hunting. I include some suggestions on how to find a good outfitter, if you are looking for a guided hunt.

The book is based on my forty years of elk hunting experiences. Over that period of time, I have been very fortunate to have taken thirty-five elk - thirty-three bulls and two cows. Almost all the elk I have shot have been at a range less than fifty yards, many at less than twenty-five yards. I have taken only one at a range greater than a hundred yards.

The book is not a "brag sheet" of my elk hunting prowess or successes, but rather a catalog of the many mistakes I made over the years, how I learned (sometimes slowly) from all of those mistakes and how I improved my knowledge of elk, my hunting style, my hunting techniques and ultimately, my success at hunting elk.

I am not a trophy hunter. I have never scored a set of antlers from a bull that I have shot. Antler score is not important to me. I consider every elk I have ever taken as a gift from nature (or, as we say in our hunting camp, a gift from the "hunting gods").

All the elk hunting I have done has been on public land (mostly on the White River National Forest) in the central Colorado Rockies. I will describe and refer often to the area where I hunt, but for reasons that many readers will understand, I cannot reveal the precise location. The area is simply described as "Mountain A, Mountain B and Mountain C." This is a string of mountains running east to west, separated by deep draws. The elevation along the crest of these mountains is between 10,000 and 11,000 feet. The terrain is heavily forested with expansive stands of aspen and intermittent stands of mixed conifer trees. Along the south side of the three mountains, at lower elevation, are subsidiary finger ridges and draws.

I have dressed, quartered and packed out myself on foot every elk I have ever shot. In our hunting area, there are few roads and the steep, heavily timbered and rugged terrain makes access on

ATV type vehicles impossible (a good thing …). Because of these factors, there are elk in the area. Nearly all our hunting is done on the downhill flanks of the three mountains. Any elk taken must be packed on foot uphill back to camp.

For virtually my entire elk hunting career, I have hunted with my sturdy and dedicated hunting partner Fred H. Fred grew up in Maine in a "hunting family." He is a skilled outdoorsman and is the most persevering person I know. There is no one on the planet I would rather have with me in a difficult situation. I refer to him often throughout this book. About ten years ago, Fred's two sons, Fred Jr. and Mike, joined up and are members of our elk hunting camp. Fred has taken about the same number of elk over the years as I have, although he's taken a few more cows than I have shot, and Fred Jr. and Mike have taken another half dozen or so animals between them.

Throughout this book, I will often refer to the term "having a shot." Having a shot means that (a) you have a clear line of fire to your target (i.e., an elk) and (b) you have a high degree of confidence that you can place the bullet you fire in a vital area of the animal. If both of these criteria are not met, you do not have a shot and you should not shoot.

There is a significant difference between "having a shot" and "taking a shot." Taking a shot does not involve a high degree of confidence in placing your bullet in a vital area on the animal. It only involves the possibility of hitting the animal. Shooting when you only have a possibility of hitting the animal will result in a missed shot or worse (much worse …), a wounded animal. To shoot when you do not "have a shot" is unethical and entirely contrary to fair chase hunting practices (more on this in the chapter titled "Hunting Ethics").

I frequently use the terms elk and animals interchangeably. They mean the same thing in this book. I also frequently use the term "heavy timber." This means the dense stands of conifer trees in the area where we hunt, mostly lodgepole pine, fir and spruce trees. Other terms are sometimes used for these conifer stands such as "black timber" or "dark timber." These terms also all mean the same thing.

The first chapter is titled "Finding a Place to Hunt," which I feel is an appropriate starting point. In that chapter I refer to various state Fish and Game departments, all of which officially have different names (e.g., Colorado: Colorado Parks & Wildlife; Montana: Montana Department of Fish, Wildlife and Parks; Wyoming: Wyoming Game & Fish Department). For simplicity, I will refer to any of them simply as a "Fish & Game" department. For the sake of brevity, I do not mention all the other western states' Fish & Game Departments where elk are found. No disrespect in any way is meant by not mentioning them by name. They are all as outstanding as those that I do mention.

Similarly, in the first chapter I discuss a process of finding an outfitter for a guided hunt, in the event that this is something you have an interest in doing. I mention outfitters and guide associations and licensing boards in the states of CO, MT and WY. Again, for the sake of brevity, I have not mentioned those in the other elk hunting states. Please recognize that there are many first class outfitters in the other states as well.

In the chapter titled "Elk Hunting Gear – Getting Equipped," I make recommendations on various elk hunting gear ranging from binoculars and rifle scopes to clothing, boots and other useful hunting items. My recommendations are my own and are based solely on my direct, real world hunting experience –

what I have found that has worked for me. For the record, I have received no direct or indirect compensation or consideration for any item recommended (no free hunting trips, no free samples, no discounts – no quid pro quo of any kind). In certain instances, my views undoubtedly reflect biases that I have developed over the years based on my hunting experiences.

The antlers on all the bulls mentioned in this book are counted on a western count basis. Elk are located primarily in the western states and western count is convention for elk. Only a complete rube refers to a five-point bull as a "ten-point." Save yourself some embarrassment and use western count for elk. (The only exception to this rule is a bull with an uneven number of tines on his antlers. If, for example, you were to shoot a bull with five points on one antler and six on the other antler, it is perfectly acceptable to describe him as a "five by six").

Some of what I write in this book, particularly in the chapter titled "Hunting Ethics" (and perhaps in the preceding paragraph), will offend some readers. I make no apology for this. I have strong views on ethical hunting practices, on fair chase hunting and on lawful hunting. My hunting companions and I adhere to the highest level of hunting ethics. One of my objectives in this book is to convince you to do the same.

Finally, the last full chapter in the book (other than the list of Final Points) is titled "Firearms/Hunting Safety." I end with this subject because it is without question the single most important aspect of hunting (and as you will see when you read the chapter, I have some personal experience in this area). I will do my best to impress upon you the absolute necessity that you and your hunting colleagues practice an uncompromising standard of firearms safety. You simply must do this – no exceptions.

I hope you enjoy this book and that you benefit from the many errors – and an outright blunder or two—that I have made over the course of my forty years of hunting elk. Hopefully, after reading it, you will not make the same mistakes I have made and will enjoy greater elk hunting success sooner than you otherwise might have.

CHAPTER 1

FINDING A
PLACE TO HUNT

One of the most fundamental aspects of elk hunting – and one of the most difficult – is finding a good place to hunt. You can hunt in a lot of places throughout the western United States (and now in a few eastern states, as well), but finding a good place to hunt, a place where there are a reasonable number of elk, where you have a reasonable chance of taking one and at a location that you can get to, is often a challenge.

WHERE TO START

The first place to start in finding a good place to hunt is to think hard about whether you have any family, friends or acquaintances that might be helpful. If, for instance, you have some relative, even a distant relative, who is a farmer, rancher or owner with property in elk country, you will want to get in touch with them (preferably through a personal visit) and see if they might let you hunt on their property. The same approach goes for any friends or acquaintances who may be able to provide you with access to an area where you could hunt.

If you are fortunate enough to have a relative, friend or acquaintance with a place in elk country, be prepared to offer some time to help with farm/ranch chores as a way of showing your appreciation for permission to hunt or providing hunting access. Farmers and ranchers typically have many more maintenance projects than they have time to do themselves. They would welcome some extra help to pare down their to-do list. Most people can handle a pick or shovel, a post hole digger and can build or mend fences. Offer to help the farmer or rancher during the summer months for a weekend or two. This is a great way to start a relationship that can last many years.

If you don't have any family, friend or acquaintance contacts, you will need to start a more systematic search for a place to hunt. Most elk in the United States are found in the western states and most of those elk live on public land, mostly on the millions of acres of National Forest land. Some areas are, of course, better than others, mostly due to better overall habitat. Most states' Fish & Game departments maintain detailed databases on estimates of elk populations, the ratio of bulls to cows and the average success rate for hunters. One of the best places to start the search process for a place to hunt is with these databases.

Ideally, you will want to focus on areas with a high estimated population of elk, a high bull to cow ratio and a high level of hunter success. If you plan to hunt with an over the counter license, be sure to also focus on those hunting units (aka Game Management Units (GMUs)) that are open to over the counter licenses. Analyzing Fish & Game databases takes time and effort and it can be quite tedious. An excellent article on this subject, titled "Where to Hunt in Montana" by Jack Ballard, was published in the 2017 September-October issue of *Montana Outdoors* magazine. The article describes a hypothetical process of winnowing through the statistical databases maintained by the Montana Department of Fish, Wildlife & Parks to identify a place to hunt in Montana. Reviewing this article, reprints of which can be obtained from the MT Dept of FWP (www.mt.gov/mtoutdoors), provides a useful example of how to navigate through the MT FWP website and is also a helpful template for working through other states' Fish and Game websites to identify places to hunt.

Like a number of other states, the Colorado Department of Parks & Wildlife maintains a database with elk population, bull/cow ratios and hunter success data. The Department has a feature on their website called "Hunt Planner." It provides a step by step guide for helping new hunters or non-resident hunters with the process of sifting through the various databases to identify GMU's with attractive elk hunting attributes. You can also call the Department and speak with someone and/or meet with them in person for personalized service (at no cost). They will help you through the process of identifying a place to hunt. Be sure to review the Hunt Planner website information first to determine things like which season you would like to hunt (there are four in Colorado as of this writing) and where in the state you might like to hunt. Having done a bit of homework prior to talking to (or meeting with) a Parks & Wildlife person will make the conversation much more productive.

In addition to the various state Fish & Game Department databases, there are commercial services that offer similar data and information, and sometimes maps and some analysis, for a fee. They are simply another alternative for searching for a hunting area.

Another good source of information lies with local game wardens (sometimes called District Wildlife Managers). Since game wardens work in defined districts, often comprised of a number of GMUs, by definition this approach means that you have already identified an area where you want to investigate potential hunting spots. It is the business of game wardens to know where the game are generally located. I have found game wardens to be without exception excellent people. They are passionate about what they do. They have a tough job enforcing fish and game laws and dealing with all manner of people, but they also have an interest in seeing hunters achieve a degree of success. They are not likely to tell you specifically "go here" or "go there." They may, however, provide some general guidance and suggestions as to places that would be worth exploring. Consider any information they provide to you as a solid lead.

One other approach to finding a place to hunt, suggested to me by a game warden friend, is to contact the Fish and Game department wildlife biologists (aka terrestrial biologists) who are usually located in district or area offices. Similar to game wardens, it is the business of these people to generally know where elk are at various times of the year, how large the herds are and what kind of shape they are in. Wildlife biologists are also not likely to direct you to a specific spot, but like game wardens, any information they provide to you should be considered a solid lead on which to follow up.

To contact a game warden or District Wildlife Manager or wildlife biologist, you will need to first contact the state Fish & Game department or locate the contact information on a Fish & Game department's website like Colorado's Hunting Atlas. There you can identify the name and contact number (sometimes you can get E-Mail addresses too) for the game warden (and sometimes the wildlife biologist) responsible for the area you are interested in investigating. Start with an introductory phone call or E-Mail and try to arrange to meet the game warden personally. Some wardens will be willing to meet with you and some won't. For those that are willing to spend a little time with you personally, this usually means meeting up with them in their office (i.e., their truck) at a convenient location during their less busy time of year – usually the winter or spring months. Don't contact them in the weeks leading up to the start of the hunting season(s). Game wardens, even during their relatively less active periods (there is rarely a "slow" period), are still very busy. So be patient in getting a response if you call or E-Mail them. I have never had a game warden not return a phone call, although it was sometimes a week later. If you are not able to meet up with them in person due to their (or your) schedule, a phone call conversation will have to suffice. When you do talk or meet with them be sure to be organized and prepared. They will be much more responsive to you if you don't waste their time.

One more option, at least in Colorado, is what is called the Ranching for Wildlife (RFW) program. This program provides Colorado residents with the opportunity to hunt on private ranch land normally closed to the public. Participating ranches provide public hunting access to their ranches free of charge to those who draw licenses under the RFW program. Other western states have similar programs. The Colorado RFW program is very popular and it usually takes at least five preference points to obtain one of the coveted licenses.

In Colorado, there is also an extensive Youth Hunting program available. This program is designed to introduce young people to hunting through extended hunting seasons that provide young people ages 12 – 17 with more opportunity to fill a hunting license that remains unfilled during the regular hunting season. This can be a great way to encourage and mentor a son or daughter, a nephew or other young person to become involved in hunting.

ACCESS, ALTITUDE AND BEING PREPARED

The process of identifying places to hunt, involves more than contacting relatives or friends in "elk country," digging through state Fish & Game statistical data or trying to talk or meet with a game warden or two. Access is also a key consideration. Will you be able to get to the area where you want to hunt at the time you plan to go hunting ?

Our elk camp is located at 10,600 feet and the route into the area cannot be called a road. It is barely a "Jeep Trail" and I have often thought it would be a challenge for a WWII half-track, particularly after it has snowed. Many times, Fred and I have had to chain up all four wheels of our pickups in order to get in (as well as get out). The route is characterized by deep mud holes, oil pan busting rocks, extreme ruts, slick slopes, narrow paths through trees and all manner of other hazards. Driving in to our camp on this track is often an hour long, white knuckle, tight sphincter ride. One particularly challenging spot, which we call the "Rock Pile", is a steep, rock choked hill. In dry conditions it is tough and in wet conditions, it is extremely hazardous. I have had to winch my rig up it on more than a few occasions.

The point of this description is that you need to know what you are getting into in terms of access and you need to think realistically about what you and your vehicle can handle. If your vehicle is stock, low clearance SUV type vehicle, you will be limited as to where you can go. You would be crazy taking a stock SUV on a route like the one we take. Taking a rental vehicle into the back country ? Forget it. You need to know your back country driving capabilities as well as your vehicle's capabilities and limitations before heading into the back country.

Google Earth maps can be helpful in evaluating access, but it is best if you can visit your prospective hunting area off season, before you head in to hunt. Doing some off -season access reconnaissance can be combined with some pre-season scouting. The more you know, the better off you will be and the better prepared you will be when you go in to hunt. If you are not able to visit the area you intend to hunt, call the Forest Service (if you are on National Forest lands) and speak to one of the resource people about access to the area that you intend to visit. They will know the roads in the area and should be able to provide you with some information on their condition. Going in blind is fraught with risk.

Fred and I have encountered other hunters while driving into or out of our camp over the years who have stopped to ask us where they can buy tire chains. The time to get equipped with chains is not when you are in the back country trying to bull your way up a muddy, rutted road. Get prepared in advance and prepare for the worst. (It is always helpful to know how to put chains on properly before having to put them on in the field.) Better to have chains (and other gear, such as shovels, an axe, tow straps and a Hi-Lift jack) and not need them, than need chains and other gear and not have them. Getting stuck or going off a mountain road can be supremely inconvenient and it goes without saying that it can really eat into your hunting time.

Another consideration is altitude. If your home is at an elevation of 1,000 feet and you are going to say, Colorado, and will be hunting at 9,000 or 10,000 feet, you had better think about how you are going to deal with that altitude difference. You will need to prepare for the thinner air environment in which you will find yourself when you arrive at your hunting destination. The last thing you want is to be afflicted by the headaches, lethargy and nausea of altitude sickness when you are hunting.

Symptoms of altitude sickness (aka Acute Mountain Sickness or "AMS") vary and range from mild at elevations of 5,000 – 6,000 feet to more severe at 9,000 – 10,000 feet. Usually they start with headaches and fatigue, but can include dizziness, nausea, trouble sleeping and flu-like symptoms. Severe cases of altitude sickness (rare at most hunting altitudes), can cause more intense symptoms that can affect your heart, lungs, muscles and nervous system. More severe symptoms like these will require medical attention.

Altitude sickness is caused by fewer molecules of oxygen being present in the air at higher elevations than at lower elevations. In order to maintain a level percentage of oxygen in your blood, you breathe at a higher rate at 10,000 feet than you do at say, sea level. The higher breathing rate expels water from your body in the form of vapor, which results in dehydration. It is estimated that twice as much water vapor is expelled at 6,000 feet than at sea level, resulting in an additional quart of water loss from your body each day. At higher elevations, the rate of dehydration is commensurately higher. Dehydration can be quite debilitating. Symptoms are similar to altitude sickness and include muscle fatigue, dizziness, reduced cognitive processing, a confused or dazed state of awareness and of course, thirst. I have experienced dehydration first hand and believe me, it is nothing to trifle with.

Being afflicted with altitude sickness and/or dehydration, even mildly, can really impair your ability to hunt effectively. You certainly don't want to spend the first day or two of your limited hunting time lying in your tent trying to catch up on the acclimation process. If you are coming from a lower elevation area and you plan to hunt at a much higher elevation, there are two things you can do to combat the effects of being at a higher altitude. First, try to arrive at your hunting camp a couple of days prior to the start of your hunt. Plan to do some hiking (which can double as scouting) to help acclimate yourself. Just spending a couple of days (the more days the better) at higher elevation will go a long way toward acclimating you to the higher altitude and decreasing the effects of altitude sickness. Second, drink plenty of water. Increasing your intake of water helps to mitigate the impact of a higher breathing rate at altitude and resultant dehydration. Minimize or moderate your alcohol intake as it contributes to dehydration.

I have experienced this issue myself. In the mid-1980's, I moved from Colorado to the East coast for a job in New York. I continued to go out to Colorado each Fall to hunt elk. Going straight from essentially sea level to our elk camp at 10,600 feet was a real bear and I suffered mightily from altitude sickness for the first several days of hunting. I eventually found that if I traveled to Denver (elevation 5280 feet) on business for a couple of days prior to heading up to our elk camp (which I could usually arrange to do), the effects of the altitude differential were much less. Getting in a light work-out, a bike ride or a run while in Denver made the elevation transition even easier.

Access considerations and altitude are clearly factors that you need to take into account when you evaluate potential areas to hunt. If you plan to hunt in November toward the end of the seasons in Colorado, for example, you will likely encounter snowy conditions. This may limit your access to certain higher elevation areas. If you choose to hunt one of the earlier seasons in October, snow may not be as big a concern (but be prepared for it). Fred and I have literally been snowed out of our elk camp in mid-October on a few occasions.

Another point related to finding a place to hunt is your physical condition. Elk hunting is a physically demanding activity. Elk are usually found in rugged, high and mountainous terrain. Depending on your hunting style, there is usually a good deal of walking and hiking involved. In my experience, you are not likely to find an elk from the seat of your pickup or ATV. A general rule of thumb for elk is that they will stay at least one-half mile to a mile away from any road with regular vehicle or ATV traffic. You are doing yourself a serious disservice if you hunt from any type of machine and you are unlikely to have much hunting success. If you want to be a successful elk hunter, you will have to get out and hunt on foot.

For this reason, you need to be in decent physical shape to hunt effectively. Once again, preparation is the key. You don't have to embark on a SEAL team workout program, but setting aside some time to work out three or four times a week in the months leading up to your hunting trip will pay large dividends for you when you actually hunt.

Starting about Labor Day every September, I embark on my elk hunting physical fitness program. When I belonged to a gym, I would put a twenty-five pound barbell in a day pack, pick up an eight pound steel exercise bar to simulate carrying a rifle and climb onto a Stairmaster for at least twenty minutes. I found this to be an excellent way to prepare for the hiking when I hunted. Two or three times a week, I would add a packing hike where I would put an eighty pound bag of Quikrete cement from Home Depot on my pack frame and hike for forty-five minutes or so on nearby Open Space trails. This is the best exercise I have found to prepare for packing out elk quarters.

If you don't have a gym available, you can invent other ways to get into shape. I have a long driveway where I live that goes down a slope to my house and barn. One exercise I do now is fill a wheelbarrow about half full with gravel (dirt or rocks would work too) and push it up my driveway for about a hundred-fifty yards, turn around and go back down (without stopping). It takes me about five minutes to do one round trip and I do this five times with about a thirty second rest in between trips. Each week I add a shovel full more of gravel to keep it challenging. It's a pretty good workout for your legs, arms, core and aerobic capacity.

Similarly, you can put some weights in a backpack, cut a piece of half inch steel pipe down to a length that weighs about eight pounds and hike at a steady pace in a park or Open Space area. You are really just limited by your imagination in what you do - but you should do something to prepare for the physical demands of hunting. You will not regret it.

When you have zeroed in on a place to hunt, do yourself a favor and get a decent hunting map of the area. The ones that I have found to be the best are called DIY Hunting Maps (www.DIYHuntingMaps.com). These maps are similar to USGS topographic maps, but with a lot more information on them. Like the USGS maps, they show topographic contours, prominent mountains, roads, trails and lakes, rivers and streams. They also show (color coded) land ownership, what land is private and which is public (National Forest, BLM, State lands), information which is very helpful to a hunter. The maps are organized by Game Management Unit, often combining several GMU's in one map (front and back). Currently, DIY Hunting Maps are available for Colorado and Wyoming, with Montana available soon.

I find the DIY Hunting Maps to be far more helpful than the app type maps that can be obtained for your phone or on GPS devices. The phone app and GPS maps are fine for showing your path from point A to point B, but to me, not so helpful for showing information on a larger scale. I would much rather look a large paper map to plan my hunting strategy than a thumbnail portion of that map on a 2 inch by 4-inch screen on a phone or handheld GPS unit.

THE OUTFITTER OPTION

Signing up to hunt with an outfitter is clearly another option for someone who does not know where to go. It is the outfitter's job to have done all the research outlined above and get you into good elk country. Most outfitters are quality people, highly motivated to get their clients in front of an elk. A few are fly-by-night outfits, interested only in taking your money. Think of the outfitter as a sort of General Manager. He has all the camp equipment and manages a group of guides, whom he has hired to take clients out to hunt. Sometimes he will guide hunters too. The guides often act as wranglers to look after the horses, if it is a horse operation. Most guided hunts will have a camp cook (sometimes the outfitter's wife or a relative).

As with most endeavors, you have to put some effort into choosing a reputable outfitter. One place to start is with a company like Cabela's, which screens and qualifies outfitters before endorsing them. Even with an endorsement from a company like Cabela's though, you need to do some due diligence to determine if the particular outfitter is the right "fit" for you (and vice versa). For example, if you are allergic to horses, you would probably want to choose an outfitter that does not use them (be prepared to do quite a bit of hiking instead). Alternatively, if you are in poor physical shape or have a physical impairment, traveling by horse might be ideal.

In most states, outfitters must be licensed by the state and most are members of state outfitters organizations like the Colorado Outfitters Association, the Montana Outfitters & Guides Association and the Wyoming Outfitters & Guides Association. The various state guide associations have websites where members of the association advertise their businesses and services. This information can help you determine if a particular outfitter is what you are looking for in a guided hunt. The state licensing board websites can also be useful, as you can check there to confirm that the outfitter you are interested in using is licensed. The licensing board websites also contain a list of any complaints filed against outfitters (for Colorado, Montana and Wyoming they are: Colorado Office of Outfitters Registration; Montana Outfitters & Guides Licensing Board; Wyoming Outfitters Board). If you are considering a guided hunt, it is worth checking both the guide association websites and the state licensing board websites. It's all part of your due diligence process.

When you have narrowed your search to two or three potential outfitters, it is time to give them a call. Do this well in advance of the hunting season, otherwise you may find the outfitter is full or can offer only a few fill-in dates that may or may not work for your schedule. Ask some practical questions: How many other hunters will be in camp?; What are the accommodations like?; What is the terrain like where you will be hunting?; Will you be hunting on public or private land? ; How to do get around (horses, vehicles, hiking)?; Who does the cooking and what are typical meals like?; What is the typical daily schedule like (e.g., do you hunt from dawn to dusk or just morning and evening)?; What is the ratio of guides to clients? Be sure to confirm that the outfitter is licensed by their respective state outfitting board.

An obvious question to ask any outfitter is what is the average success rate for his hunters. Few outfitters can claim a 100% success rate and if one were to make such a claim, I would be very suspicious. You will want to ask for some references from prior clients. The outfitter will likely provide you with the names and contact information of clients that have had successful hunting experiences. Be sure to ask for some names and contact information for clients who were not successful, too. (In fact, I would suggest asking for more of those than the successful clients.) Talking with former clients, both the successful and unsuccessful ones is far better than relying on ratings you may find on the internet.

Another source of outfitter information are the various sportsmen's shows that are held each year around the country.

One of the biggest is the "Hunter's Convention" put on annually by Safari Club International, usually in Reno, NV. The one I am most familiar with is the International Sportsmen's Expo that occurs every January in Denver, CO. (International Sportsmen's Expo shows are also held in Sacramento, CA, Salt Lake City, UT and Scottsdale AZ.) Most of these sportsmen's shows are a showcase venue for outfitter and guiding services. The advantage of going to one of them is that you have the opportunity to meet outfitters personally, talk with them, ask questions and determine if their particular hunt is the right one for you. This is not a substitute for performing your due diligence on the outfitter though. Consider a personal conversation as a better substitute for the phone call you would otherwise make. Still ask for references and check out the outfitter on their respective outfitters & guide association and state licensing board websites.

Recognize that the outfitters with booths at the sportsmen's shows are there trolling for clients and there is probably an incentive for them to tell you what they think you want to hear. Any outfitter that gives you a hard sell such as "You better sign up now, or there might not be a spot for you" is a sign for caution. Also, recognize that there are lots of other outfitters and guides that have solid businesses that are not at the various outdoor shows. You can find them by checking state outfitters and guide association websites or by looking through the outfitter advertisements in the Rocky Mountain Elk Foundation's magazine, *Bugle*.

The most common complaint I have heard from every outfitter I have ever known concerns the poor physical shape of most of their clients. Face it, whatever type of outfitter you choose, there will be some walking and hiking involved. The last thing a hard working guide wants is to put a client in front of a nice bull elk and have the client blow the shot because he is panting and wheezing so much he can't hold his rifle steady. Do yourself (and your guide) a favor and make an effort to prepare yourself for some physical activity if you are out of shape. You will enjoy the hunting experience much more that way.

Similarly, if you have signed up for a hunt where you will be riding horses and riding is not something with which you are familiar, it would be a good idea to take a couple of riding lessons at a local horse facility before you leave for the hunt. This does not mean that you need to become an accomplished equestrian, but it clearly would be helpful if you knew how to comfortably mount and dismount from a horse, put on a halter and a bridle and (ideally ...) could saddle and unsaddle a horse. These are not complicated skills and can easily be learned with a couple of lessons. Granted, these are generally things the guide is responsible for, but having a rudimentary knowledge of how to deal with a horse is good to have in the event of a bad storm, a horse wreck on the trail or an emergency situation (such as your guide getting injured after being bucked off by a spooked horse - it happens). Having just some minimal knowledge of horses and riding will make the riding experience much easier and more enjoyable. Once again, be prepared.

HOW WE FOUND A PLACE TO HUNT

When my hunting partner Fred and I started the process of trying to find a place to hunt in the late 1970's, there were no statistical data bases, Google Earth maps or other sources of information to help narrow our search. It was a trial and error, boots on the ground type of approach. The first year, Fred hunted elk in the Rabbit Ears Pass area near Steamboat Springs, CO. I spent time in the Sleepy Cat Trail area outside of Meeker, CO, evaluating the area for elk hunting potential.

We eventually decided to focus on areas within about a three-hour drive of Denver, where we both lived. The first year was a sort of "exploratory" year where we tried several different areas. One area we hunted had a lot of elk sign, but was quite difficult to access, requiring a long 1-2 mile uphill hike. Even though there were clearly animals in the area, we decided to abandon it due to the difficult access situation.

Another area we investigated also had serious access issues. Like the first area, we observed plenty of elk sign, but we ultimately decided to discard it due to the problematic access (mostly due to a very steep Jeep trail into the area and the prospect that we would not be able to get in (or out) in rough weather).

We finally decided to focus our efforts and time on a third area. This is the area I described in the Introduction as "Mountain A, Mountain B and Mountain C." As described earlier, the access can be quite difficult, but properly prepared, at least it was do-able.

This area is heavily forested with an expansive mix of aspen and conifer trees. The pine, spruce and fir trees provide cover and security areas for the elk, while the aspen stands provide feeding areas. There is adequate water available for the animals. Each year we would take one or two "scouting" trips and roam around, noting where we bumped into elk and where they went when they ran off. Over time, we learned the nuances of the terrain, where it made sense to hunt and where we should probably not hunt due to topography, pressure from other hunters or distance from our camp. We basically began a long process of what I call "learning the area."

For about the first ten years, Fred and I would pack in a backpack type camp a mile or so down to the base of Mountain B. We would pre-position some food and water there before the season started and then walk in with our hunting gear and rifles the day before the season opened. Looking back on those years, I can't believe we did what we did, sleeping in a tiny backpacking tent and cooking on a minuscule little stove in all kinds of weather. It was like special forces training.

Later, in the early 1990's, I invested in a 12 x 14 foot canvas wall tent from Montana Canvas in Belgrade, MT and we moved our camping location to the top of Mountain B. Now we could drive right to the tent spot and bring in much more gear. Over the years, this developed into what became a relatively comfortable camping set up, far more luxurious than our primitive backpacking camp of the early years. Instead of sleeping on a thin foam pad, now we had cots. What a difference that made! Another standout feature of our new accommodations was that we could hang wet or damp clothing from the ridge pole inside the tent and get it dry. This was a big improvement over our previous elk camp housing arrangement. There were lots of other upgrades also, like a vastly improved stove for cooking, that made the elk camp experience a lot more comfortable.

We have remained at this camping location for the rest of our hunting seasons, now running on 30 years. Staying in this one area has allowed us to really expand our knowledge of our hunting area. Learning and knowing your hunting area is, in my view, a key success factor in elk hunting.

Our elk camp at the top of Mountain B

The process of learning your hunting area takes a lot of time – years, in fact. Each year you accumulate a little more data about where the elk are, where they might be and where they might go when pushed. Gradually, over a period of time, you can gain insights into the elk behavior and habits in the area. As you accumulate more experience, observations, successes and failures, you build an inventory of data on the elk and the area which allows you to increase the odds of locating and taking an animal.

Fred and I have gained a lot of insight about our area over a forty year period. When we first began hunting in the Mountain A, B and C area, it was mostly a sort of random walk type of hunting. We both roamed around from dawn to dusk, bumping into animals here and there, hoping to have a shot. We did shoot some animals, but the randomness of the way we were hunting left a lot of room for improvement.

Each succeeding year, we learned a little more. We saw where the elk tended to go when we "bumped" them. We quickly learned that gently "bumping" the animals was far preferable to blundering into them and spooking them. When we bumped some elk, they tended to move off a few hundred yards and could often be followed, even without snow on the ground. With a very careful approach, this sometimes afforded the opportunity for a shot, sometimes not. Most of the time, we would only get one "bump." After that, the animals would spook and would be gone.

We learned to take advantage of other hunters' activity, positioning ourselves in places where elk might come by us after having been bumped or spooked by another hunter. We learned about the dense pine, fir and spruce stands where the elk would often bed down during the day. Some of these stands of heavy timber were quite small, like little isolated "islands" in the larger stands of aspens. We also learned about areas that other hunters, probably for reasons of difficult topography, seemed to avoid. Because these areas remained largely undisturbed by hunters, they would occasionally contain bands or groups of animals, sometimes bedded down out in the open in the aspen groves.

Over the years, we also identified general routes and networks of trails the elk tended to use when traveling from one area to another. One thing we noted was that if animals were spooked by other hunters over on Mountain A, they would often run down into the deep draw separating Mountains A and B, and move over to Mountain B. Similarly, if we or someone else spooked animals on Mountain B, they tended to run over to Mountain C or over to Mountain A, depending on the direction of the wind.

In the mid-1990's, I built a small tree stand in the aspens on a slight inflection point on the side of Mountain B, about a half mile from our camp. The location afforded a view of trails that elk used both uphill and the downhill from the tree stand. Over time, I realized that this spot was on a general elk travel route from Mountain A. If hunters there spooked a bunch of elk, the animals would often come over to Mountain B and move past the tree stand spot, either above or below it. Elk also tended to move past this spot as they traveled across Mountain B, from the west. In addition, animals would sometimes come down from the top or come up from the bottom of Mountain B, past the tree stand. I eventually realized that the tree stand spot was in fact, an intersection of elk travel routes and it proved to be a highly productive place from which to hunt.

Fred located a similar spot about half a mile away in a broad, shallow basin full of aspen trees, near the base of Mountain B. This was a place that seemed to be ignored by most other hunt-

ers and it became clear to us that the elk felt comfortable and secure there. Like my tree stand spot, elk would move through this area and sometimes they would bed down there. It also proved to be a highly productive place to hunt.

Fred and I began to hunt off our respective spots, me in the tree stand and he in the aspen grove, in the mornings. If no elk materialized, we would often move to the

My tree stand on Mountain B

various stands of heavy timber and look for animals there. Some of these heavy timber areas also became stand spots where we would sit during the afternoon. One small, narrow strip of heavy timber, not far, but a thousand feet downhill from our camp, became another very productive spot because we found that it was largely ignored by other hunters and that elk traveled through it and bedded down in it on fairly regular basis. We would go to this spot sometimes in the afternoons. It eventually became known as the "afternoon stand."

Learning your hunting area takes a lot of time. However, if you are able to return to the same area year after year and spend the time and make the effort to learn it, the body of knowledge you develop will give you a significantly improved chance of taking elk there. One of the best examples of this I experienced was one opening morning when I was on my little tree stand on the slope of Mountain B. This particular year, Fred's son, Mike, was sitting in Fred's aspen grove spot, west and downhill from me, toward the base of Mountain B.

Around 9 AM or so, I heard some commotion above me, breaking branches and the sound of approaching spooked elk. I immediately grabbed my rifle and swiveled around to face uphill. A few seconds later a large cow came barreling down through the aspen trees directly at me, followed by a group of about a dozen more animals. The cow stopped about twenty-five yards uphill, which put her on the same visual plane as me. She stared straight at me for about thirty seconds and then turned ninety degrees, facing west. During this time, other animals had drifted down through the aspen trees uphill from her and I saw that the group included a nice five-point bull. There were a lot of eyes on me and I dared not to move a muscle – I sat absolutely still. I just watched as the elk slowly followed the moves of the lead cow and began to move on contour along the side of the slope, twenty-five to thirty yards uphill from me. When I felt the time was right, I raised my rifle, preparing to shoot at the bull (I had a solid shot at him). As I did that, another, larger five-point bull came into view up the slope at the tail end of the group. Two big bulls in the small band elk – I was amazed. I shifted my attention to the larger bull. He stopped about thirty yards away, with his vial area obscured by several aspen trees. The other elk were moving away, but he remained motionless. My rifle was up and I was aimed at him, but I did not have a shot due to the trees partially blocking him. I was panicky that he would suddenly trot or run forward to catch up with the rest of the animals, now about twenty yards away from him. He did not run though. He took a step forward providing a clear line of fire to his heart/lung area and I fired.

At the sound of my shot, the rest of the elk bolted to the west, angling downhill. About five minutes later, I heard a shot from the direction of Fred's aspen grove stand where his son Mike was sitting. I learned that evening when I was back at camp that the same band of elk that had come by me, had run down past Mike after I had shot the second bull in the group. Mike had shot the other bull, the one I had seen initially. It was a rough morning for the elk that day, but a good one for us, thanks in part to our knowing our area. There was no way to actually know that the elk would run down to where Mike was sitting, but knowing that the elk liked that spot, there was reasonable chance that they would.

Another time, I was sitting on the afternoon stand, having hunted over to it after there hadn't been any action on my tree stand. The afternoon stand is located in a thin strip of heavy timber on the steep south facing slope of Mountain B. The spot where I sit is between two very large spruce trees and has a good view down through the timber below into the bottom of a heavily timbered draw. Eight hundred yards away is a long finger ridge which forms the other side of the draw. At about 2 PM, I heard a shot from the opposite side of the draw. I knew from previous experience at this spot, that if animals were spooked on the other side of the draw, they were likely to head over to the side where I was sitting. I got ready and had my rifle in my hands, anticipating that some elk might show up.

About ten minutes after the shot, I saw some movement through the timber about a hundred and fifty yards away, down in the bottom of the draw. I immediately began scrutinizing the spot with my binoculars. A large cow elk materialized, followed by more animals. The elk, numbering about twenty cows, calves and several spike bulls, slowly and in complete silence, filed like ghosts diagonally up the slope through the dark timber below me. I searched for a large bull, but did not see one in the group of elk. I concluded that the shot I had heard from the other side of the draw must have taken the large bull in this group of elk. I had a cow tag and since it was the third day of hunting for us, I decided that I would now use it. Almost all the elk had passed by me, except for a few more cows. I picked out the last one and was preparing to shoot when I noticed a slight bit of movement downslope from the direction from which the animals had come. I held my fire on the cow and looked more carefully down through the timber. A large bull, walking very slowly, a good twenty-five yards behind the last cow, came into view through the timber. I waited until I had a clear line of fire and was confident about my shot. When he was about forty yards away, I fired. He turned out to be a fine six-point bull.

I have always attributed this success to our knowledge of our hunting area. I can recall that in our early years of hunting, I would occasionally hunt through this area but I never recognized its potential until years later when I shot a bedded down bull there one morning. After that, I paid a lot more attention to this little strip of timber, eventually realizing that it was a place that the elk really liked. I have probably taken nearly a dozen animals from this spot over the years. This kind of knowledge does not come in just a visit or two to an area (at least it did not come to me that fast ...) It takes time, but putting in that time to learn your area can dramatically improve your odds for success.

CHAPTER 2

KNOWING YOUR QUARRY

A SHORT HISTORY OF ELK

When the first European settlers arrived on the shores of the North American continent, elk populations were estimated to have numbered 10 million animals, spanning virtually the entire width of the continent from the Atlantic coast to the Pacific coast (see Figure I). The American Elk is the second largest member of the deer species in North America (after moose). They were called "wapiti" by Native Americans, a word meaning "white rump," that is still commonly used today to describe elk.

Unregulated hunting and relentless westward expansion by settlers, coupled with urban and agricultural development and

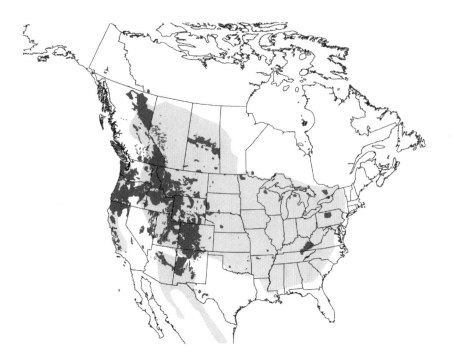

Figure 1. Historical elk range (light gray) and current elk range (dark gray).

loss of habitat throughout the nineteenth century, resulted in the extirpation of elk east of the Mississippi by the late 1800's. These factors are estimated to have (incredibly) reduced elk populations from their original 10 million animals to less than 100,000 animals continent-wide by the early 1900's. Surviving elk populations were squeezed into relatively small, remote areas in the Rocky Mountains and the Cascade Range.

In the early 1900's, conservation efforts were initiated to reverse the decline in elk populations. Through a combination of regulated hunting, concentrated wildlife management efforts along with the elk's ability to adapt to a variety of habitats and food, elk populations began to stabilize and, in some areas, rebound.

Today, four subspecies of elk live in North America. A small population of Tule elk (estimated at around 3000 animals), a subspecies in California, is managed by state and federal agencies on California public lands. The Manitoba elk is a subspecies that once ranged across the great plains area east of the Rocky Mountains in Canada and the United States. Now, they comprise about 20,000 animals located mostly in provincial and national parks in Manitoba and eastern Saskatchewan. The Roosevelt elk, a Pacific coast subspecies estimated to number about 100,000 animals, ranges from northern California to Washington and into Canada. The largest elk subspecies population in North America is the Rocky Mountain elk, numbering around 900,000 animals. They occupy mountain ranges east of the Cascades through the various smaller ranges that comprise the Rocky Mountains. Small pockets of animals have also spread into plains areas east of the Rocky Mountain Front Range (Colorado in fact, has a plains elk season.) Because they are very adaptable and can survive on a variable diet, Rocky Mountain elk have been successfully reintroduced into historical habitats in a number of midwestern and eastern states.

Elk are a great conservation success story. Reduced from about 10 million animals to about 100,000, they now number around a million or so. Their rebound is a tribute to a concerted conservation effort by many wildlife conservationists and state and federal wildlife agencies. It is only because of their collective efforts that we have the opportunity to hunt elk today.

In recent times, an organization founded in 1984 by four Troy, MT hunters, the Rocky Mountain Elk Foundation (RMEF), has contributed mightily to expanding and enhancing elk habitat and elk hunting opportunities. The RMEF's mission is to ensure the future of elk, and other wildlife, their habitat and our hunting heritage. The RMEF is the leading organization focused on conserving, restoring and enhancing natural habitats, promoting sound management of wild elk and restoring elk to their native ranges. The organization is also involved in educating its members and the public about habitat conservation and our hunting heritage.

The RMEF has protected and enhanced over 7.3 million acres of land and has been involved in opening and/or securing access for hunting and other outdoor recreation on more than 1.2 million acres. The RMEF has also been at the forefront of restoring elk to former native ranges. It has worked with state Fish & Game departments to reintroduce elk to suitable areas in eleven eastern and midwestern states, including Arkansas, Kentucky, Michigan, Tennessee and Pennsylvania.

The RMEF is a great conservation organization and I urge you to join it. As mentioned in the previous chapter, they publish a magazine called *Bugle*, which contains excellent articles about elk and elk hunting. The outstanding magazine itself is easily worth the modest cost of membership in the RMEF.

ELK AND THE WIND

I once read many years ago, probably in an article about elk hunting in one of the "hook & bullet" magazines, the dogmatic statement that "elk always travel into the wind." I can tell you with equal dogmatism that this statement is absolutely untrue.

In my experience, elk travel about 50% of the time into the wind, about 30% of the time across the wind and about 20% with the wind. I think it is certainly true that elk prefer to travel into the wind since their sense of smell is so important in detecting danger. However, there are situations, for instance when they want to move from point A to point B, when the wind is not in an ideal orientation for them. When that happens, they may have to travel with the wind blowing across them. They also travel with the wind, more often than you might think.

Thermal air currents are an important feature of hunting in mountain terrain. In each twenty four hour period, air in the mountains cools at night. Since cool air is heavier than warm air, cool air moves downhill starting in the late afternoon or early evening and continues that way until the next morning. In the morning, as the air warms it begins flowing uphill. Elk take advantage of these air currents when they move. Often (but not always ...) they will move to higher elevations during the evening when the thermals are flowing downslope, so they can detect any danger through their sense of smell on the way up. Then, in the morning, when the air is warming and the thermal flow changes to upslope, they will tend to move from higher elevations to lower elevations so they can detect danger on the way down. Sometimes animals will remain at a higher elevation in a spot where they can take advantage of the daytime uphill thermal flow to detect danger below them.

Because thermals are important to elk, they are also important to an elk hunter. If for example you are approaching a strip of heavy timber on the side of a mountain at, say mid-day, you will want to approach it from the top, so your scent flows away from any elk that may be located below you. If you approach from the bottom, your scent will flow up through the timber, to any elk that are there and warn them of your approach.

Thermals are important and you need to pay attention to them. When I first started elk hunting, I was not very savvy about them, which no doubt worked to my detriment. Over the years, I have become quite a student of the thermals. Now, for instance, I know that the thermals will change from downslope to upslope around 9 AM on Mountain B and change from upslope to downslope at about 4 PM. It's helpful to know the thermals in your hunting area so that you can hunt in a manner that will avoid alerting animals to your scent. Thermals can sometimes help alert you to the presence of nearby animals by bringing their pungent, barn yard sort of smell to you. Any time I get a whiff of the smell of elk, I go on high alert as they are usually only two or three hundred yards away.

Something that I did to remind me of thermal air currents was to attach a strand of orange thread I pulled from my Filson hunting vest to the front sling swivel on my rifle. I call this my "Windicator." It's not really to detect wind. You will know whether the wind is blowing or not or whether or not there is a breeze. However, I have found that simple strand of thread to be a helpful indicator of thermals and other slight, almost imperceptible air movements. It is also a constant, helpful reminder

The Windicator on my rifle

to me to be aware of air movements all the time. I know, you may think this is a silly little accoutrement. Perhaps it is – all I can say is that it works for me.

One of the things I have found surprising about elk is how often they move with the wind, i.e., with the wind at their backs. The largest bull I have ever shot, a really large bodied, heavy beamed six-point, happened in the first ten minutes of the season one opening day morning. I got a little bit of a late start from our camp that day and arrived at my tree stand later than I intended, around 7 AM, just as it was getting light, about ten or fifteen minutes later than I normally did. There was a light breeze blowing from the west, so when I got settled on the stand, I sat facing to the east, expecting any animals that approached would appear from that direction, heading into the wind.

When I am sitting on the stand, I am seated between the trunks of two large aspen trees. The trunk of the tree on the right obscures my field of view in that direction. At about 7:10 AM, I heard the sound of a twig snapping off to my right, out of view. I leaned back to look around the aspen tree trunk and there, twenty yards away, was a group of half a dozen or so cows coming along a trail that passed right by the tree stand. I remember being disappointed that there was no bull in the group. I returned to my sitting position and as I did, a huge bull walked slowly and silently into view below me, about fifteen yards downslope. He had been obscured by the aspen tree trunk next to me. My rifle was leaning up against the tree trunk beside me and I slowly moved my arm to get it into my hands. I was petrified that he (or the cows) would see the movement of me bringing my rifle to bear, but I managed to do it without alerting him. He was a monster.

There were a number of unusual things about this experience. First, I arrived on the tree stand a little late that morning, but fortunately (downright luckily, in fact), I got there just before the elk arrived. Second, the animals were heading east, with the wind behind them. I was expecting that any elk would approach from the east, heading into the breeze that was blowing out of the west, so I was not looking to the west. Third, this group of animals got within about twenty yards of me before I detected them by hearing the twig snapping. Finally, in contrast to most situations, the bull was out in front of the group of elk - typically, they bring up the rear. My position, about twelve feet above him on the tree stand, probably saved me from being spotted by him or the cows when I moved to bring up my rifle. I was not so fortunate with another bull, to be described later.

I think one of the lessons from this experience is that there are no hard and fast rules when it comes to elk. There are certain general guidelines, but the animals can, and do, surprise you from time to time. Also, this experience reinforced the need to arrive at your hunting spot in the dark, not at or after daybreak. It also demonstrated that elk can approach from any direction, regardless of wind direction and they can approach silently.

It never ceases to amaze me how an animal roughly the size of my fifteen-hand quarter horse, Fritz, can move among aspen trees and through heavy timber in absolute silence. Somehow, elk can and I see them do this every year that I hunt. Fritz is an exceptional mountain horse. He is very smart and can handle just about any back county situation calmly and safely, but if I rode him in any of the places where we hunt, you would hear us coming two hundred yards away. The ground all around the tree stand in every direction for hundreds of yards is littered with dead aspen leaves. Walking through them is like walking through a field of corn flakes. Yet elk can move through them in complete silence. With elk's ability to move through terrain in silence, you cannot rely on your hearing to alert you to their approach. You must rely primarily on your eyes. Depending on your hunting style (more on this in chapter 4), this is a very important thing to keep in mind when elk hunting.

A couple of years later, on another opening morning, I was back on my trusty tree stand. We had listened to the weather report the evening before on our little weather radio that received National Weather Service forecasts and learned that a snowstorm was headed our way. The forecast said it would begin snowing at 8 AM the next day. I always take the forecasts as a rough estimate because so many times they are off, sometimes way off. I noted it, but did not really think too much about it.

I was on the stand before daylight. Nothing happened for the first hour, but at precisely 8 AM, flakes of snow started to drift down. An hour later, it had developed into a full-blown snowstorm and at about 10 AM, I decided it was time to pack it in. (It did not help that I was not properly dressed for the snow due to my weather forecast skepticism – another lesson learned.) At this point, there was a good five inches of snow on the ground. I hiked up to a game trail about three hundred yards uphill from the stand and headed back to camp.

The snow was coming down hard and visibility was only fifty yards or so, with the snow blowing in from the west, the direction in which I was headed. I was about halfway back to camp when I happened to glance downhill toward a gap between some large spruce trees and I was amazed to see a nice five-point bull walking along about forty yards below me on a reciprocal course, headed east, with the wind behind him. If I was going to have a shot, I was going to have to move fast, because the opening that he was passing through was only about twenty-five yards wide.

I quickly pulled off my trigger hand glove with my teeth, dropped my pack so I was better balanced, flipped open my scope covers, dialed down my scope to some lower power, threw the gun to my shoulder, aimed just behind his shoulder and fired. The bull stopped and just stood there. I was stunned that he showed absolutely no reaction to the shot. At the sound of me working the bolt to chamber another round, he wheeled around and bolted back in the direction from which he had come.

I raced down to where he had been standing to check for evidence of a hit. There was none. I followed his tracks in the snow for a good three or four hundred yards, without finding any evidence of having hit him. I finally concluded that I had missed. I couldn't believe it. In fact, a good ten years after it happened, I still can't believe I missed that shot (as you can probably tell, I still haven't gotten over this ...) Thinking about it later – and often – I decided that in my rush to shoot, I must have somehow shot over him. I can't figure out any other reason for the missed shot. At least it was a clean miss.

Sometimes things just don't work out. The lesson here is that a rushed shot – and that shot was rushed – is probably a poor shot. This bull is also another example of an animal that was moving along with the wind at his back.

I have encountered many elk that act in ways contrary to convention. One more account of animals moving with the wind behind them may convince you that these are not some sort of anomalous occurrences.

Another year, I was sitting at a spot in a stand of heavy timber we came to call the "Skull" because we found an old elk skull nearby. It overlooks a saddle between two draws and we had seen elk travel through the area on numerous occasions.

A breeze was blowing once again from the west and I was positioned facing downhill and east, expecting any approaching animals to come from that direction. It had snowed about three inches the night before and a light snow was still falling that morning. Around 10 AM or so, I was surprised to suddenly pick up the strong, pungent smell of elk. I realized that they could only be upwind of me, to the west, and that they must be close. I slowly shifted my position and looked to my right, and there, probably only twenty yards away, was a small group of elk approaching, almost on the same contour on which I was sitting. I also saw that there was a bull, walking along on a parallel course with the other elk (all cows), about ten yards further downslope. I was trying to figure out how I was going have a shot at the bull, given the proximity of the cows. It seemed to be an impossible situation, but I remained absolutely motionless, doing my best to become one with the tree I was sitting against. Incredibly, the cows filed slowly past me, about twenty feet away. The bull lagged a little bit behind the cows and I thought it best to let him walk past me and then shoot from slightly behind him. The bull walked slowly by about ten or twelve yards away. When I raised my rifle, he saw the movement and lurched forward into run just as I squeezed the trigger. I could tell from blood on the snow that I had hit him, but I was concerned about the location of the hit, given his sudden movement just as I fired.

I followed his tracks, which were intermingled with those of the cows. Alarmingly, there was no blood trail in the snow. I followed the tracks for about a hundred and fifty yards to a point where all the tracks except one set, deviated down toward the saddle below. I guessed and hoped that the single set of tracks were those of the bull and decided to follow them. I followed the tracks into an aspen grove off the saddle. There, about a hundred yards away, I spotted the bull. He was bedded down and when he saw me at a distance of about seventy-five yards, he got up, but did not move off. I fired another shot from about sixty yards and he went down. I discovered when I dressed him out that my first shot had gone diagonally through him, entering just behind the diaphragm on his left side and then traveling through his right lung, exiting just behind his right shoulder. I have always considered this particular animal to have been a close call for me. While it was an OK hit, if there had not been snow on the ground, it would have been difficult determining where the bull had gone and I might have had a long search to find him. I am very glad that was not the outcome.

A noteworthy aspect of this experience, other than this being another example of elk moving with the wind rather than into it, is the traveling position of the bull relative to the group of cows. This bull, like the largest one I shot described earlier, was in an offset position relative to the other animals. Both of the bulls were ten to fifteen yards away, downslope from the cows with which they were traveling. I have noticed this positioning often enough that I have come to call it an "outrigger position." You can probably only note this positioning arrangement if there is snow on the ground, but if you come across it, it is a serious clue that there is a bull in the group of elk that left the tracks.

Having this knowledge really paid off one year for me. I was hunting along a long, heavily timbered finger ridge down at the base of Mountain B. There was about three inches of fresh snow on the ground. I was hoping to cut an elk track trail and in late morning, I did. From the number of tracks, I estimated that a group of eight or ten animals had moved along the ridge.

Significantly, there was an "outrigger" track, set five to ten yards off to the side of the rest of the tracks. That gave me reason to suspect that a bull was with the group of elk.

I followed the tracks for about a quarter of a mile, constantly glassing ahead with my binoculars to see if I could locate the animals before they saw me. (More about glassing ahead in a following section.) The tracks continued along the low ridge to a spot where it bordered a broad, shallow aspen basin where they turned down into the basin. I could see a long distance through all the aspen trees and I stopped and started glassing the entire area. There, at least four hundred yards away, was the group of elk. They were all bedded down, except for a spike bull that was about two hundred yards away, grazing through the trees. The large bull that I suspected was with the group was bedded down by himself, about twenty-five yards from the cows.

I sat down and tried to analyze how I was going to get a shot at the bull. The range was, to me, excessive and I did not want to risk shooting at a four hundred plus yard distance, at a bedded down animal, through a maze of aspen trees. In other words, I did not have a shot.

The grazing spike was another problem. He was about halfway between me and the rest of the elk. He was a kind of roving sentry and if he spotted me, he would spook and take the other animals with him. I considered backtracking and making a sort of end run around the top of the aspen basin to come in from another direction. A light breeze was blowing from the west though, and I felt there was too much risk that the elk would scent me.

I finally decided that my best option was to try to close the range and try to find a favorable spot from which to take the best shot I could. I got down on my hands and knees and started crawling through the three-foot-tall grass among the aspen trees. Every ten yards or so, I would stop and slowly raise my head above the grass, periscope like, to check on the spike. I did that for about ninety yards and finally got to a position where I did not feel I could go any further for fear that the spike would spot me.

I crawled around and found a downed aspen tree trunk in a spot where I had some cover from the spike and could stretch out prone. It provided a view through the trees that gave me a clear line of fire to the bedded bull. I took off my pack and laid it in front of me as a rest for my rifle. I felt I had a shot - a clear line of fire to the bull and I believed I could land my bullet in his heart/lung area, even though he was bedded down and the target area was smaller. I took probably five minutes setting up to shoot, but I finally squeezed the trigger.

At the sound of the shot, the rest of the elk all bolted. I chambered another round in my rifle and noted that the bull had stood up, but was not moving away. Now I had a standing, broadside shot at him, and I fired again. He went down. Both shots turned out to be lung shots. They are the longest shots I have ever taken at an elk – about 325 yards.

One lesson here is that the outrigger track configuration offered a significant clue that a bull was in the group of elk. With that information, I followed the tracks in a careful manner and when I finally found the animals, I was able to make an extremely cautious approach to a spot where I had a shot. Crawling for almost a hundred yards was necessary to avoid detection by the grazing spike bull. In elk hunting, sometimes you have to think outside of the box a bit and use unconventional methods.

SCENT CONTROL

It is well known that elk use their sense of smell as one of their main tools to detect danger. In our early years of hunting, while Fred and I were busy learning our hunting area, I made one mistake after another in mis-gauging, being careless about the wind or sometimes just plain ignoring wind direction. I blew many opportunities for a shot at animals because of my crude hunting practices. What I saw more often than not were those "white rumps" of the elk disappearing into the timber out ahead of me.

One particularly hard scent lesson I experienced occurred one day when I was carefully approaching a small section of heavy timber. I was making every effort to approach in my best "stealth" mode. I had glassed ahead with my binoculars and saw that there was a group of animals bedded down in the timber. A light breeze was in my face and the elk had not detected me. The set up looked perfect and I was excited at the prospect of having a shot at an animal. When I was about seventy-five yards away from the elk, there was a sudden back pulse of the breeze and for about ten seconds or so, it blew back towards the elk. Almost instantly, the elk began getting off their beds and a few seconds later, they took off down the hillside crashing through branches as they made their getaway. The last animal I saw was a large bull, running downhill through the heavy timber.

Another year I was over on Mountain A sitting at a spot at mid-day above a strip of heavy timber hoping that some elk might wander by. At about 12:30 PM, I saw some movement a couple of hundred yards to the south. A group of about eight elk emerged from the aspens. They were all cows and I only had a bull tag. I sat there and watched them walk slowly along contour about fifty yards above me. When the lead cow entered my scent plume, flowing uphill on the thermals, she turned around and with the other animals, bolted back in the direction from which the elk had come.

The following day, I went back to the same area but moved about seventy-five yards further upslope. Amazingly, around noon or so, a group of elk suddenly appeared off to the south again. This time there was a bull in the group, trailing the last cow by about thirty yards. The problem was the elk were even further upslope from where I was now sitting and when the lead cow entered my scent plume flowing uphill on the thermal flow, she turned and bolted, taking all the elk with her. There was no chance for a shot at the bull. My lack of scent control measures was really costing me opportunities for having a shot at an animal.

Being the persevering hunter that I am, I went back to the same spot again the next day, moved even higher upslope and waited for some elk to come by again. No animals appeared.

A year or two later, shortly after I had built my small tree stand, I was sitting there opening morning with high hopes for the season. A light breeze was blowing from the west, so I positioned myself looking east, expecting that any elk would approach from that direction. About an hour after daybreak, I saw some movement about a hundred and fifty yards away to the east, near a stand of heavy timber. A large cow elk had stepped out from the conifer trees and came to a dead stop. I could see a large group of animals backed up behind her in the trees. She stood there for about thirty seconds staring straight in my direction. I realized then that my scent was being carried by the breeze directly to her. Suddenly, she turned ninety degrees and headed straight downhill at a run. The rest of the elk, probably twenty-five animals, followed suit. I was crushed to see at least two good bulls in the group. There was no opportunity for a shot, with the animals running through the dense stand of aspen trees. Another blown opportunity. Despite these types of setbacks however, one way or another, probably through sheer perseverance, Fred and I each managed to get an elk most seasons.

After suffering through numerous other mishaps like these, I finally decided there had to be a better way and I decided to get serious about scent control. I started using commercially available scent control sprays and I used scent control soap before heading out to hunt. These measures seemed to be somewhat effective, but not entirely. I was still being defeated on a regular basis by the elk's sense of smell (and my poor hunting practices).

About that time, I read in some elk hunting article about a guy who advocated taking alfalfa tablets prior to hunting as a way to reduce your human scent (basically to make you smell more like grass...). I had read somewhere else about the importance of airing out your hunting clothing prior to heading out to hunt. I am certainly no "granola head" and I have to admit that I thought the alfalfa tablet thing was bit out there, but I decided to give it a try. In addition, as part of my new mission to control my scent, I decided to also air out my hunting clothes for a couple of weeks prior to heading out to our elk camp.

About a month prior to hunting season, I began taking six to eight alfalfa tablets at each meal (and sometimes before going to bed). While I sometimes forgot to do this before every meal initially, I got better at it over time, largely by leaving an alfalfa tablet container on the counter at home and on my desk at work. About two weeks before the season, I pulled out most of my hunting clothing and hung them on a porch railing at my home.

This included the long underwear, pants, shirts and jackets that I thought I might wear while hunting. The day before I left to go hunting, I collected everything and headed up to our elk camp (along with my supply of alfalfa tablets). At elk camp, I pulled out the clothing I planned to wear and hung it up on nails I put in trees around our tent. I made sure I did not wear any of it around camp while we set up the camp and got organized. Since I am the camp cook, I was also careful not to wear any of my hunting clothing while drumming up our fine elk camp cuisine. I also continued to use scent sprays. (The one I came to like the best, and still use, is Dead Down Wind.) The next morning, opening day, I headed out to my tree stand. A light, intermittent breeze was blowing from the west. At about 8 AM, a nice five-point bull appeared to the east, probably bumped by someone over on Mountain A. He was headed in my direction, moving along a trail about 50 yards below me, so I was not too concerned about my scent flowing to him. As he neared me though, the breeze stopped and the downhill thermals took over, taking my scent downhill directly to him. He walked calmly right through my scent plume and never showed the slightest indication that he had picked up my scent. When I had a solid shot opportunity through the aspens, I fired.

I was pretty happy with this scent experience, but I have to admit, I thought that it might have been some kind of fluke. Maybe the downhill thermals had not taken my scent to the bull as I thought they had. My elk camp mates were certainly skeptical too. I did not worry about it too much though and based on that experience, I decided to adopt the alfalfa tablet/clothing airing program for the future.

The following year, I followed the same scent control protocol, duly consuming alfalfa tablets in the weeks preceding the hunting season opener and airing out my hunting clothing. The only change I made was in addition to spraying the Dead Down Wind spray on my clothes, I also started spraying it directly on my skin before putting on my hunting clothing. Opening morning was a dud that year and I headed over to the afternoon stand to sit for a couple of hours in the heavy timber during the mid-day period. There was no breeze, but the thermals were strong, heading directly upslope from where I was sitting. At about 1 PM, I heard some crashing and breaking of branches to my east and uphill, the sounds of approaching spooked elk. I had been facing downhill, but swiveled partially around and got my rifle in my hands just in time to see a group of about eight cows angling down the slope through the aspens. I could tell that they would cross above me about twenty-five yards away. They slowed to a walk as they reached the heavy timber and moved along contour just above me. Now I saw that a good bull brought up the rear of the group. The lead cow stopped directly above me, turned her head and stared at me for a good twenty seconds or so. I dared not make the slightest movement (but I was able to dial my scope down with my thumb to the lowest power for the short range). My scent was blowing directly to her on the uphill thermal air flow.

She did not show any indication of concern and after standing there another minute, she started to move off at a slow walk. The other cows followed one by one, each walking directly through my scent plume being carried to them by the uphill thermal. I still had not moved. The bull held back a bit and was partially obscured by some trees. When the cows had moved on another ten yards or so, the bull started to walk forward. When his head passed behind a tree trunk, I chanced bringing up my rifle, hoping the movement would not be seen by the cows. They did not spot it and when the bull cleared the tree, I had a solid shot and fired.

I was really pleased with this experience because it confirmed to me that my scent control program actually worked. Fred, in his conservative Maine style, still did not seem convinced, but so be it, I believed I had hit on a winning formula for controlling my scent.

From that point on, I used this system (which I dubbed the "Cleveland Scent Control Program") with great success. I have not, to my knowledge, been detected by an elk's nose since I began using it. I have many other examples of it having worked, all similar to the experiences described above. I can't claim that this "program" will be as effective for you, but frankly, I know of no reason why it would not (unless you are a smoker – it might not work then). You may think it is nonsense. That's fine – all I can say is it works for me. By way of summary, you need to:

1. Start taking alfalfa tablets three or four weeks, at every meal, before you go hunting

2. Two or three weeks before you go hunting, hang your clothes outside

3. Before you go hunting, shower with a scent controlling soap

4. While traveling to your hunting spot/camp, do not wear your hunting clothes

5. At the end of each hunting day, change into other clothes and hang your hunting clothes outside

6. Use a scent controlling spray (I think application directly to your skin is most effective.)

I think it is also a good idea to store your hunting clothes separately from your regular clothing off season. I keep all my hunting clothing in large, resealable plastic bags (the ones with the slider tab closure are the best). This way, your hunting clothing is not exposed to other odors while in storage. Plastic storage boxes with sealable tops are also a good way to store hunting clothing.

I also always wash long underwear, T-shirts and other similar washable type clothing in Dead Down Wind laundry detergent. I hang these items out for the two or three week period along with my other hunting clothing prior to hunting season too.

Never travel in your hunting clothing. I am always surprised when I see guys in the airport during the fall on their way to hunt outfitted from head to toe in their camo hunting pants, shirts and jackets like they are about to head out hunting. That clothing, if it is the same clothing they intend to wear when they actually do head out to hunt, will be full of all manner of odors that will surely alarm any elk. Better to pack your hunting clothing in resealable plastic bags in your luggage and wear non-hunting clothing when you travel.

I have come to believe that controlling your scent is not doing just one thing, but rather doing a number of things in combination. It is clear to me that just using a scent spray product or just washing with a scent suppressing soap is not enough. I have found that scent spray, washing with scent suppressing soap, using the alfalfa tablets, plus the other measures discussed above together can have a meaningful impact on controlling your scent. Yes, it is a bit of a nuisance, but if you are really serious about addressing the scent issue, it is worth the effort. All I can say, is that it has worked for me – really worked.

THE NOSE KNOWS, AND SO DO THE EYES

While it is certainly true that elk rely heavily on their sense of smell to detect danger, I have found that an elk's sense of sight is an equally important tool to detect danger.

My hunting partner, Fred, and I both agree that a critical success factor in hunting elk is seeing the elk before they see you. Seeing the animals first gives you time to get set up for a shot and thereby avoid a rushed shot. Having time to set up and take your shot with care will result in greater elk hunting success for you and help you avoid wounding an animal.

It goes without saying that if elk see you moving through the woods, they will be alerted and will likely spook. I have found elk to be much more sensitive to movement than deer. If deer spot you moving, they will often stand around and watch you, sometimes for several minutes. If you then stop moving, they will often slowly wander off or continue on their way. This rarely happens with elk. If they spot you moving, they will almost always spook.

I have observed that there is something about arm motion in particular that really upsets elk. Early on when I would spot some animals, I would raise my binoculars to look more closely at them and to see if one was a bull. If the elk saw that motion, they would almost always bolt, even when the wind was in my favor. Raising my rifle to my shoulder would often have the same result. Over time, I learned to be much more prudent and careful in how and when I moved my arms.

One year I was hiking up the side of Mountain B in the middle of the day when I spotted a long line of elk walking along contour, headed west into a light breeze, about eighty yards above me. I watched them for half a minute or so and then slowly brought my binoculars up to scan the line to see if there was a bull in the group. There was, back toward to end of the line. I was slowly bringing down my binoculars with my left arm and slowly bringing my rifle up with my right arm, when suddenly the animals took off, thundering away in full spooked mode. I knew they had not scented me. They could only have seen that arm motion. Another lost opportunity.

One of my biggest blunders (perhaps the single biggest) was one year when I had stopped at the afternoon stand to have lunch and sit for an hour or two. It had been a slow morning and I was probably not at my most alert level. It was around 2 PM when all of a sudden, a four-point bull appeared, all of ten yards away, having approached from my left in complete silence. He stopped and stood in full view right in front of me. The thermals were upslope at this time of day, so there was no chance that he could smell me. (This predated my scent control program.) Instead of letting him move on a few more yards to a spot where a couple of trees would have blocked his view of me, for some reason I started moving my right hand and arm toward my rifle (it was leaning against a tree next to me). The bull stood there stock still. I got my hand on the gun and as I was slowly raising it to my shoulder, he (predictably) bolted down the slope and was gone in a couple of seconds. To this day, I cannot figure out why I did that – it was so dumb! The thing that made the whole experience particularly aggravating was that I knew better. An incredibly foolish mistake and another lost opportunity.

This was a hard lesson, but it was one that I really learned from. It really hammered home to me that elk are very intolerant of movement. I have found that elk will spook just as frequently if they see you move as if they scent you. I have thought of elk's sense of smell as a kind of long-range radar because they can pick up your scent out of visual range and evade you. Their eyesight is like a short-range radar. In my experience, if they see you moving, even if they have not scented you, they will bolt.

One year I was hunting in a thick strip of heavy timber over on Mountain A. This particular strip of timber was well known to us as a place where the elk liked to bed down during the day. It is very thick, with a tangled mess of blowdowns throughout from top to bottom.

It was mid-day, with the thermals flowing upslope. I approached the timber section near the top to take advantage of the thermal flow, creeping along a game trail in my best stealth mode. I entered a particularly thick section of the timber and paused to scan the area downslope to see if I could locate a bedded animal. As I studied the almost impenetrable mess of downed and leaning trees, I noticed some of the branches in one blowdown spot, about forty yards below me, were moving around. I gradually realized that I was looking at the antlers of a bedded down bull. I stood there watching the antlers congratulating myself on having made such a good approach and trying to figure out how I was going to get a shot at this animal.

Suddenly, as if you had pulled an ejection seat lever, the bull leaped in a single bound up and over the blowdown tangle and disappeared downhill. It all happened literally in the blink of an eye. I stood there, dumbfounded. While this bull could not have scented me, he had clearly seen me (and probably heard me). The movement of his antlers was him preparing to make his exit. I still don't know how I could have approached this animal in a way that would have afforded a shot. Maybe this needs to be a two man hunting spot, one person up high to move any elk there and another, downslope to try to get a shot. Needless to say, this section of heavy timber is a pretty safe place for the elk.

Another movement mistake concerns how you carry your rifle while you hunt. You should always carry your rifle in your hands. Don't carry it slung on your shoulder. The motion of moving your arms to unsling your rifle off your shoulder is easily picked up by elk and if they see it, your opportunity for a shot will likely be gone. There is a natural inclination to carry your rifle on your shoulder, particularly when you have walked a long time and have not come across any animals. It takes discipline to overcome this practice. After experiencing many blown opportunities resulting from elk spotting the movement of unslinging my rifle, I finally started forcing myself not to carry my rifle on my shoulder. If I got tired of carrying my rifle in my hands, I would stop for a few minutes, sometimes longer, and rest. I told myself that as soon as I slung my rifle, I would run into elk (this actually happened quite a few times). Think of it this way: if you have your rifle slung on your shoulder and you come upon some animals, you are essentially doubling the risk of detection, once by unslinging the rifle and again by raising your rifle to your shoulder. There is a lot of arm motion in those movements. Time is of the essence when you spot some animals and need to focus on having a shot. Unslinging your rifle is unnecessary movement which can result in being spotted by the animals and losing the opportunity for a shot. If you can train yourself to carry your rifle in your hands, you will be a more successful elk hunter.

The take away here is that you really need to be careful with your movement. If you can spot the animals before they see you, you will have a great advantage. If they see you first, they will have the advantage and it will probably be difficult to have a shot. Be particularly careful with arm movement, it really tends to spook elk. If an elk surprises you at close range, you need to freeze and only move when the animal cannot see you (like when its head is behind a tree trunk). Do not make the foolish mistake I made. Never make any movement when the animal has eyes on you.

GLASSING AHEAD

Because elk are so sensitive to movement and so attuned to detecting it, it is critical to spot them before they see you. I have learned that the single most effective way to do this is to do what I call "glassing ahead." If you learn nothing else from this book, let it be this one hunting technique. It will significantly increase your chances of taking an elk because it will allow you to locate the elk, in many instances before the elk locate you, thereby allowing you to get into a position where you can have a shot.

Glassing ahead is an easy thing to describe, but is a hard thing to actually do. Glassing ahead is the practice of using your binoculars to scan each new section of cover or terrain as you move through the woods. There is a natural inclination for hunters to use their unaided eyes to look for elk as they hunt. Glassing ahead takes effort (although, not much...) and many hunters would rather just rely on their natural eyesight. The problem with this approach is that elk are difficult to see, sometimes even when they are close by. They have excellent camouflage, keen noses and eyesight and excellent hearing. Their ability to detect you is, for the most part, better than your ability to detect them.

Even if you get a handle on controlling your scent (with the Cleveland Scent Control Program, of course), you still need to have a way of dealing with the elk's excellent eyesight and sensitivity to movement. The way to do this is to get in the habit of always glassing ahead. This allows you to spot animals at longer ranges and in difficult cover. It allows you to spot standing and slowly moving animals so that you don't blunder into them and blow an otherwise good opportunity to have a shot. Glassing ahead really helps in locating bedded animals because they are very difficult to spot with natural eyesight. Unless you glass ahead, a bedded down elk in cover will almost always spot you before you see them.

Getting into the habit of glassing ahead is not easy. In our early years of hunting, during the "random walk" period, I would routinely bump into groups of animals, sometimes bedded animals, often at relatively short ranges, fifty yards or so, that would run off (the white rump syndrome). One example of this occurred one afternoon while I was slowly making my way back to camp. I had covered a lot of ground that day without having seen a thing and by the time I started heading up through a timbered slope to a ridge above, I was pretty beat. The area I was moving through was mostly mixed conifer trees, but relatively open and easy to move through. I trudged along, sometimes looking at the ground in front of me, rather than looking ahead for any elk. About a third of the way to the top, I suddenly spotted a cow standing about fifty yards away. As I looked at her, I noticed more and more elk getting up through the trees. A group of about twenty animals was bedded down there. As the animals started running downhill, I frantically began searching for a bull. I finally saw him, a large five or six point. He was one of the last to go, but running down the hillside through all those trees did not offer the opportunity for a shot.

After blowing one opportunity after another like that over the years, I became determined to find a way to not bungle so many opportunities. I realized that the way I was using my binoculars was to look at animals after I had spotted them with my natural eyesight, but almost always *after* they had already seen me and were moving off. It finally dawned on me that I was using my binoculars completely backwards—I should be using them to try to spot the animals *before* they spotted me.

I started forcing myself to glass ahead each time I approached a new section of cover. If it was a section of heavy timber, I would often spend several minutes studying the area to try to see if I could find an elk hidden among the trees and blowdowns. In more open areas, like the aspens we hunt in, a quicker glass ahead scan can often suffice. I found that if I scanned ahead, I could spot the animals early and could often get into a position to have a shot. It worked.

One of my early successes glassing ahead, and one that really confirmed to me that it was worth the little bit of extra effort involved, occurred late one morning on the second day of an elk season. I had been sitting on the Skull stand, watching the saddle down below it, but there had been no activity. Around 10:30 AM, I decided to go over and check out a small section of heavy timber on a steep hillside a quarter of a mile or so away. I hunted my way slowly and deliberately over to the heavy timber spot, always glassing ahead. As I approached the area, I paused about seventy-five yards away and spent several minutes looking carefully among the trees with my binoculars. I saw some bedded down elk. I moved closer very slowly, concerned about not alerting the animals. When I was about fifty yards away, I spotted a nice five-point bull. He was bedded down thirty yards or so away from the rest of the elk, further upslope. On my hands and knees, I slowly maneuvered to a spot where I had a shot. When I fired, the rest of the animals, about fifteen in all, bolted downhill. The bull got up, went about five yards and went down.

It was clear to me that had I not glassed ahead, I would likely not have had that opportunity. I would have run into the elk for sure, but they would have all been running full tilt downhill and there would have been no chance for a shot. (I never shoot at a running elk. There is never a shot at an elk running through heavy timber.)

After this experience, I became a confirmed practitioner of glassing ahead. It has proven to be my single most valuable elk hunting technique and has proven to be particularly helpful in spotting bedded animals. To me, there is no greater success than taking a bedded down bull at close range. I think of it as a sort of high achievement in elk hunting.

One thing elk do that is good to know, related to the two examples discussed above, concerns how they arrange themselves when they bed down on a hillside. I have found that when a group of elk bed down on a slope, they are arrayed in a rough tear drop shape, with the wide section of the teardrop lower on the hillside and the tip of the teardrop on the higher part of the hillside. I have also found that any bull in the group will always be at the top end of the elk disposition (i.e., the "tip" of the teardrop). For this reason, when I encounter a group of bedded animals on a slope, I immediately start searching for a bull toward the top of the elk "formation" and don't waste time looking through all of the animals lower down. This was the case in the two glassing ahead examples discussed above and I have never seen this not to be the case. Since time is of the essence when you find a group of bedded down elk, don't waste time looking for a bull where he is not likely to be. Focus on the top of the group first thing – that's where you will find him.

Another common characteristic of elk is that if they are in a group or herd, they will almost always be led by a cow. This is because this is the animal with the "knowledge." This is the animal whose job it is to detect danger. She is also the animal that best knows the trails and routes, knows best the terrain, knows best where to go in the event of danger and undoubtedly knows all manner of other things critical to elk survival. If you were on a military infantry patrol, the lead cow would be the equivalent of the "point man." If you are hunting with a cow tag, never, ever, shoot the lead cow. In my view, killing that particular animal results in great harm to that group or herd of elk by taking out the animal on whom the rest of the animals rely for safety and survival. If you are shooting a cow, always select one other than the lead cow.

Similarly, I would never shoot a cow traveling with her calf. I had a friend in Montana do this once. The calf hung around thirty yards or so away the entire time that he dressed out, skinned and quartered the cow, all the while crying, baying and squealing for its mother. He told me that he found the experience so traumatic that he would never do it again.

I have always thought that shooting a cow with a calf probably condemns that calf to death. I doubt that it has the skills and knowledge to survive. Most elk country is rife with predators, mountain lions, bears, coyotes and in some areas, wolves. A clueless calf would be very easy prey. Shooting a cow that has a calf with it is clearly an individual decision. For me, it is an easy decision, I will look for another elk.

CHAPTER 3

ELK HUNTING GEAR — GETTING EQUIPPED

In order to hunt elk effectively, you need to be properly equipped. Being properly equipped involves a lot of things, such as clothing, footwear, firearms and ammunition, optics and a host of other items.

In this chapter, I will discuss what I feel, based on my experience, are the essential items for elk hunting. With a couple of exceptions, everything I mention or recommend is something that I have used myself and is an item that has proven itself in the field. I will also say that some of what I recommend no doubt reflects my own biases and preferences. By way of example, I have a slight preference for wool clothing over synthetics, although I have and hunt in both types of clothing. This reflects a personal preference on my part and I am not trying to "sell" you on wool over other materials. It is just what I happen to like. What I will do though, is try to warn you away from materials that I do not think are the best choices for hunting elk. I have not tried every elk hunting product on the market, so I can only opine on those that I have tried or used myself.

As I mentioned in the Introduction, I have not received any compensation or consideration, direct or indirect, for anything that I recommend here. No free hunting trips, no free samples, no discounts or special deals – no quid pro quo of any kind. The manufacturers or retailers of products that I mention will not know of my recommendations unless they read this book (or someone who reads the book tells them). My recommendations are based solely on my own personal experience with what has worked for me over my forty years of elk hunting.

As a general statement on elk hunting gear, I recommend buying the best equipment you can afford. Buying a cheap pair of binoculars that will not stand up to the rigors of hunting (e.g., getting banged around; getting dropped; snow/rain; large changes in temperature) will not serve you well in the field. Trying to glass ahead with a pair of fogged up binoculars will negate the purpose of glassing ahead and serve no useful purpose.

Similarly, buying a cheap pair of boots, in my view, is always a big mistake. Boots get a serious workout in elk country and a poorly made pair will not stand up to hard use in mountainous terrain and variable mountain weather. Trying to hunt when your feet are cold or wet makes for a really tough day and seriously detracts from your ability to hunt effectively.

Getting equipped does not have to happen all at once. In my case, I slowly built up my inventory of hunting gear and equipment over a period of many years. If you are just starting out, in addition to your rifle, I would focus on investing in the best pair of binoculars and the best pair of boots you can afford. The rest of your gear can be added as you go. Year end sales, close outs, inventory clearances and other types of promotions, many of which occur throughout the year, can be good times to pick up really good gear at affordable prices.

BINOCULARS

In the previous chapter, I discussed the practice of glassing ahead and why I believe it is a critically important thing to do when you hunt. In order to do this effectively, you need to have a good pair of binoculars.

I actually consider binoculars to be the single most important tool you have when you hunt. I think of them as your primary weapon, more important than your rifle. Before you can use your rifle, you have to have a target and the best way to find that target is by glassing ahead with binoculars (and yes, I will continue to hammer away on glassing ahead ...). Once you find some elk, you will also probably need to identify whether or not there is a legal animal for you to shoot. Where Fred and I hunt in Colorado, a legal bull must have at least four points on one antler or a brow tine at least five inches long. You can make this determination through your rifle scope, but it is much easier and more accurate to do with a pair of binoculars. Maybe you have a herd of animals in sight that contains several good bulls. It's a lot easier to pick out the one you want to shoot with a pair of binoculars than trying to make that decision by looking through a scope.

When I started out elk hunting in the late 1970's, there were not nearly the number of excellent hunting binoculars that there are now. I can't remember what I used in those early days, but when I saw a pair of the Swarovski SLC 8x30 binoculars in 1988 or so, I was really interested in them. I had been looking to upgrade my binoculars and was impressed with the compact design, light weight and outstanding optics of the SLC. I ended up buying a pair from Orvis for around $325. I used them for many years and still consider them to be a first class hunting optic. In the late 1990's or so, Swarovski discontinued the SLC binoculars and replaced them with the EL series. After the EL model was introduced, I picked up another pair of the SLC's for about $175 as part of an inventory clearance sale an optics retailer had. Years later, I also invested in a pair of the 8x32 EL's when they went on sale, which is what I use now. They are, in my opinion, the ideal hunting binocular.

To me, a pair of hunting binoculars needs to be of at least seven or eight power and reasonably compact and lightweight. I once had a friend who joined me to hunt deer on some property my family owns in northwest Montana. He arrived sporting a large, heavy pair of marine type 12x50 binoculars. He was quite proud of them for they were excellent quality, but I cringed at the thought of having those hanging around my neck all day. While they were certainly an excellent glass, in my view, they were not the best choice for hunting.

I have observed that the $350-$400 price range seems to be a sort of break point in binocular quality. Binoculars less than that price range seem to be of lesser quality in optics and durability and over that price range, you get a much better binocular. For this reason, I think you should expect to pay at least $350 for a decent hunting binocular. (Of course, if you can get a $500 pair on sale for

$400, all the better.) There are many good binoculars at this price level available from manufacturers like Leupold, Burris, Nikon, Vortex, Zeiss and Steiner, to name just a few. I think it is always a good idea to go somewhere where you can actually handle the binocular and compare different models from different manufacturers. You may like one better over the others because it is clearer, lighter or just because it feels better to you.

Range finders are an item that have become quite popular among hunters. The value of using a range finder is a function of the environment in which you hunt. If you hunt in an area where you can expect to encounter elk out in an open area and you can remain in a concealed position, using a range finder to help you set up your shot can definitely be helpful. On the other hand, if you hunt in thick, heavy timber where your shot will likely be at relatively short ranges, a range finder is of little use and in fact, can be detrimental because using it can consume valuable time you should be using to make your shot and the movement involved can increase the likelihood of being detected by the animals.

I have a range finder, but given the environment where we hunt, I never use it while hunting. I have found it to be most helpful as a way to develop the ability to estimate ranges with my natural eyesight. I do this by practicing with the range finder off season, ranging distances to various objects and seeing what the distance is with the range finder (it's actually kind of fun). When you do this enough, over time, you can develop a reasonably good sense of distances without relying on the range finder itself. I can estimate ranges out to about two hundred yards with pretty good accuracy now, within+/- five yards or so. I believe that when you spot animals at close range, it is better to focus on making the shot than fiddling with distractions like a range finder.

RIFLE SCOPES

Since we are talking about optics, it makes sense to comment on rifle scopes. The same comment I made at the beginning of this chapter concerning buying the best equipment you can afford certainly applies here – buy the best scope you can afford. Your scope choice should also be influenced by your hunting environment. If you are like a friend who routinely hunts above tree line and sometimes takes shots at 400 yards or more, you may want a higher power scope than what Fred and I use where we hunt in timber and most of our shots are less than 100 yards. Choose a scope that best matches the terrain where you hunt.

Over the past ten years or so, a lot of new rifle scopes have been introduced by optics manufacturers and a number of new manufacturers have entered the rifle scope market. When I first started hunting elk, scope choices were limited to names like Leupold, Weaver, Burris and Bushnell. For many years, I used a sturdy and reliable Leupold 2x7, 36mm variable scope. Later, Leupold introduced a 2.5x8, 40 mm variable that I bought, which was a distinct improvement over the 2x7 scope.

In the early 2000's other optics manufacturers, such as Swarovski, entered the rifle scope market. I became quite enamored with their Z3 model scope and eventually bought one for my .30-06. Later, when I found a good sale, I bought another one for my .35 Whelen back-up elk rifle. The ones I have are the 3x10, 42mm variables. I love them. This scope is low profile, weighs about twelve ounces and I think is about as perfect a hunting scope as you can have. It also looks right on my rifles.

I don't think you necessarily need a 50mm or 56mm objective lens variable scope, which are much larger and heavier (as well as more costly) than my Z3's. These scopes can often be dialed up to fifteen to twenty power and sometimes have gadgetry like illuminated reticles, ballistic turrets and other bells and whistles. Ballistic turrets that stick up on top and out on the sides of a scope are more of a liability on a hunting rifle than an asset, as they can be easily damaged while hunting. Remember, you are not on a sniper team here, you are hunting elk. If you can't hit the heart/lung area on an elk at two hundred yards with a nine or ten power scope, you need to spend more time at the gun range. While it is certainly true that a larger objective lens scope has greater light gathering qualities than a smaller objective lens scope, I have never, ever, encountered a situation where I felt disadvantaged by not having a large objective lens scope.

I believe the bottom line on scopes is buy the one that you like the best and buy the best that you can afford. There are so many choices now that the real problem is deciding which one to buy. Be prepared to spend at least $400-$500. You want an optic that is rugged and (like binoculars) can handle the rigors of hunting in the field. Leupold is certainly a top contender for a quality scope and they offer many different models for all manner of hunting. I think their VX line is particularly good. SIG Sauer introduced a line of rifle scopes and I think their Sierra3 BDX scope looks really good as a hunting optic. Other quality manufacturers are Burris, Vortex, Zeiss, Nikon, Kahles (expensive) and of course, Swarovski. I don't believe you can go wrong with a good quality optic from any of these companies.

ELK RIFLES

Originally, I considered skipping any discussion of elk rifles because it is a topic rife with a myriad of views, opinions and controversy, a bit like stepping into a minefield. Choosing the right rifle for elk hunting is an important decision, however, so I decided to weigh in with some comments and observations, which the reader can take or leave. The intent is not to ignite another endless debate about the best elk rifle or elk hunting caliber, but rather to pass on what has worked for me. I am just conveying the caliber of rifle that I have used with a lot of success along with a few comments on what is important when shooting an elk.

I think there are a couple of things that often get lost in the never-ending discussions and arguments about elk rifles. One of those is that the most important thing in shooting an elk is not the caliber of the rifle, but rather where you place your bullet, i.e., shot placement. The second important point, which is related to the first, is that the best rifle and caliber for you is the rifle and caliber that you can shoot the best.

Every elk I have shot, with one exception, I have shot with a .30-06. The one exception was a bull that I shot with my back-up rifle, a .35 Whelen. Both rifles are Ruger Model 77's and both have been restocked by a gunsmith in Kalispell, MT. Both are very accurate guns and easily shoot sub-minute of angle groups (or as I like to say, "dime" size groups) off the bench at 100 yards.

I am not a fan of the magnum calibers, for three main reasons. First, I just don't believe you need a magnum caliber to hunt elk. I have never experienced any problem with the lethality of my .30-06 and I just feel that a magnum is more gun than is needed. Secondly, the significant advances over the past twenty or so years in ammunition technology, including improved propellants and vastly improved bullet designs along with the wide availability of factory loaded ammunition with premium type bullets has, in my view, gone a long way toward leveling the playing field between standard rifle calibers and magnum calibers (more on this in the next section). Thirdly, there are a lot of hunters out there with .300 Win Mags, .338's, .340 Weatherby's and a host of other magnum calibers who can't really shoot them all that well. I am an ardent proponent of shooting the rifle that you can shoot the best. For some people a .338 is fine, but for a lot of others, it's just too much gun, and frankly, it's not needed for elk. Remember too, that over nine million elk were killed in the 18th and 19th centuries in North America. The people who shot all those animals were not using magnum caliber firearms. They were using smoothbore long guns and later, in the latter half of the 19th century, relatively low velocity rifled bore long guns. They got close to their target and they knew about shot placement.

Jack O'Connor, the famous gun writer and outdoorsman, was a big advocate of the .270 Win. He shot who knows how many elk with rifles in that caliber without any difficulty whatsoever. I, for one, would much rather shoot a .270 than a .338 or even a .300 Win Mag. The magnum calibers will not make you a better shot or deliver a more lethal hit than a .270, a .308 or a .30-06 (or a 7 x 57 Mauser, another one of O'Connor's favorite calibers). Again, it's not about bore size when shooting at an elk, it's about shot placement. Let me repeat that, because this is a really important point: IT IS ABOUT SHOT PLACEMENT. Delivering your bullet to the heart/lung area on an elk will put it down – period. It does not matter whether you are shooting a .270 or .338. Your target area on an elk is the heart/lung area shown on Figure 2:

Figure 2. Your target area—the hart/lung area on an elk.

Now, some of you will be jumping up and down over these comments, pointing out that at the relatively short ranges at which I have shot nearly all of my elk, I don't need a higher velocity, flatter shooting caliber that will still deliver a solid punch out 400 yards and beyond. OK, I take the point on that and I recognize full well that there is a place for magnum calibers. I happen to feel though, that they are better suited for dangerous type game rather than elk. The fact remains that a .270 Win bullet delivered to an elk's heart/lung area is just as lethal as a bullet from a .338.

One of the other problems I have with magnum calibers is that some (not all ...) of the people who shoot them seem to think that the higher velocity, flatter trajectory of magnum rounds somehow magically empowers or enables them to take long range shots, sometimes very long shots. What I have found however, is that most elk hunters, unless they are graduates of military service sniper schools or have attended one of the long-range shooting courses offered by various firearms training businesses, are simply not that good at long range shooting, particularly if they are shooting a hard recoiling magnum. Long range shots involve a host of factors that the average hunter is generally not that adept at taking into account when under pressure while preparing to shoot. These include estimating range and gauging how much to hold over the animal or how to properly adjust the scope for the range, gauging wind drift to the target and compensating for uphill or downhill shooting angle. Another issue with long range shots is that invariably there are people out there who, if the animal they have shot at does not show an indication of being hit, will not make the effort to walk that 400 or 500 yards to confirm that they in fact missed (a cardinal sin, in my view). Failing to follow up on your shot is highly unethical and furthermore is a violation of hunting laws in many states (such as Colorado).

A good friend of mine in Montana goes antelope hunting in eastern Montana every October. He has hunted there as long as I have been hunting elk. When he first started hunting antelope, he was taking long range shots routinely (with a .308), mostly hitting his target, but occasionally not. Over time, he realized that the real challenge in hunting antelope was not taking shots at them at those long ranges, but rather trying to get shots at them under 100 yards. It is the stalk, or as he puts it, the "sneak," that is the real challenge. I could not agree more with that philosophy. At the end of the day, it all depends on how you want to hunt and how challenging you want your hunt to be.

Generally speaking, long range shots don't involve nearly as much skill in stalking and game knowledge as a shorter-range shot. Who needs to worry about thermals, wind direction, arm movement, whether you hung your clothes out or whether you took your alfalfa tablets when you take a shot at an elk at 400 yards ? The answer is you don't (or certainly, not nearly as much).

If you think you will be taking longer range shots at elk (e.g., 250 yards and beyond), you will need to practice shooting at targets at that range or beyond. Not having the skill to take long range shots and not having practiced long range shooting, and then taking a long range shot at an animal is irresponsible and unethical. You will probably miss or, worst case, wound a fine elk. Scores of fine animals are wounded this way every year. If you don't have the skill and haven't practiced for a long range shot, *don't shoot*. Try to close the range to a distance where you actually have a shot and have a high probability of making a lethal hit.

Having a good sling on your rifle can be very useful in a situation where you have time to get set up with it because it can help you deliver a more accurate shot. The best sling is a simple cotton sling described by Wayne Richards, creator of an outstanding series of firearms and hunting YouTube videos at his GunBlue490 site. Wayne is a true firearms authority and his video titled "The World's Best Rifle Sling" is well worth watching.

Always keep in mind that your first shot is your best shot. Sometimes, depending on the circumstances, you will have an opportunity to have more than one shot at an animal. Your first shot is your best one though, because the animal will probably not be aware of your presence, allowing you to take careful aim at the heart/lung area. After your first shot, the animal will be alerted to your presence and will, most of the time, be moving, which presents a more difficult shooting situation. I believe that taking your time to carefully set up for the shot is an important success factor in elk hunting because it allows you to achieve the best shot placement on the animal, which is the single most important aspect of shooting an elk.

Another point related to shooting is to be sure to practice with your rifle using the same ammunition you will use when you hunt. Each year, take the time (or make the time) to go to the gun range and shoot half a box or so of your hunting loads to confirm your rifle is zeroed in, before you go hunting. You must do this every year. Never assume that since you zeroed your rifle last year, you can skip checking the zero this year. I know from personal experience that rifles can get off zero just from being carried around when hunting. They get dropped, banged on rocks, bumped into trees, jostled around in vehicles and suffer other mishaps, inadvertently, all the time. You owe it to yourself, as well as any elk you might have a shot at, to confirm each year that your gun is shooting dead on.

You also need to know the ballistics for the ammunition with which you will be hunting. I know that for my .30-06, using the Federal Trophy Bonded Bear Claw loads I hunt with, if I set my scope for two inches high at a hundred yards, the bullets will be dead on at two hundred yards and about seven inches low at three hundred yards. You need to know how your bullet will travel once it leaves your barrel in order to make accurate shots, especially if you may be taking longer range shots. Most ammunition manufacturers these days provide the ballistic information for the particular load on the ammunition box, so there is no mystery (or excuse for not knowing...) about the trajectory of the particular bullet you are firing.

So, if you are trying to choose a suitable elk rifle, think carefully about how much gun you want and what you think you would be comfortable with. Always remember that shot placement is the most important factor in shooting an elk and that the best gun for you is the one you can shoot the best. All that being said, for me, my .30-06 does the job perfectly.

AMMUNITION

Another relevant factor here is ammunition. When Fred and I first started elk hunting in the late 1970's, the bullets loaded by ammunition manufacturers were pretty straightforward, such as Core-Lokt by Remington and Silver Tip from Winchester. A handful of "premium" bullets, among them, Nosler's Partition, Speer's Grand Slam and bullets from Barnes, were available, but only for handloaders. Fred was a fan of handloading and he got me into it as a way of having a better bullet available for elk hunting.

I loaded a number of different loads for my .30-06, including 165 grain Partitions, 180 grain Partitions and 200 grain Partitions. After a few years, I decided that the 180 grain bullets were the best and I have stayed with that bullet weight from that point forward. I used the Partitions for a while, but became a bit disenchanted with them after taking several bulls and finding that the forward section of the bullet often detached from the rest of the bullet. I started handloading and using 180 grain Grand Slams and shot them for several years. Both of these bullets worked well enough, but I was always looking for something better.

In the early and mid-1990's, ammunition manufacturers began offering premium bullets in factory loads. One of the first to do this was Federal, which offered the Trophy Bonded Bear Claw and the Woodleigh Weldcore bullets. I decided to try some of the Trophy Bonded Bear Claws one year. I found they shot very well from my rifle and that they held together ("high retained weight" in bullet terminology) when hitting an elk. I have used this round now for about twenty-five years and have been very satisfied with its performance.

Since the late 1990's, bullet technology has undergone a design revolution with a large number of fine premium bullets having been introduced and factory loaded by both the major ammunition manufacturers and smaller independent manufacturers. For example, Remington began offering Swift A-Frame bullets in their factory loaded Safari line (I use these when I hunt deer in northwest Montana and they are superb); Winchester has their Fail Safe bullets (and others), Hornady and Barnes have large selections premium bullet loads for virtually any situation and smaller manufacturers like HSM offer top tier ammunition loaded with premium Berger bullets. Improved propellants, premium bullets and finer tolerances in brass shell cases have resulted in outstanding performance with factory loads.

A few years ago, Hornady introduced their Superformance line of ammunition. I read reviews about the new loads in some of the hunting magazines and how well they performed. What I read piqued my interest and even though I was thoroughly satisfied with the Trophy Bonded Bear Claws I was using, I nevertheless decided to give the new Hornady ammo a try.

I bought several boxes of 180 grain Superformance rounds loaded with the GMX bullet, a polymer tip, solid copper bullet. One September morning, I went out and shot several rounds at my target 100 yards away. To my amazement, I could not get a decent group with the Hornady rounds. I fired the entire box of twenty rounds without being able to get a satisfactory group. Later I went back out and fired four or five of my Trophy Bonded Bear Claw rounds and got my usual nice, tight group. (The lesson for me here was a bit of "if it's not broken, don't fix it".)

I believe the Hornady Superformance rounds are excellent and I do not believe there is a thing wrong with them. They just don't shoot well from my particular rifle. I don't know why that is the case, but evidently my rifle simply does not "like" that particular load. I had read and heard anecdotally about rifles "liking" and "not liking" different ammunition, but had never experienced this first hand until I tried out the Superformance loads.

The take away here is that you need to find the type of ammunition that shoots well from your rifle. As I discovered, different ammunition, even really good ammunition, can shoot differently from your gun. If you can't seem to get a good three shot group with your rifle, it may not be the rifle (or you). It could be the ammo you are shooting. Before I would blame the rifle for poor shot grouping, I would try a couple other types or brands of ammunition. If that does not show any improvement, then the problem could lie with the rifle (or the shooter).

I think the wide availability of factory ammunition loaded with excellent premium bullets has been a real game changer in elk hunting (and in fact, in all kinds of hunting). I think standard caliber ammunition loads with premium bullets have diminished the benefits of magnum calibers. You simply don't need that hard recoiling magnum cannon for elk. The standard caliber premium ammunition is just as lethal as any magnum caliber out there. Shoot the gun that you can shoot the best and always remember that the single most important thing in shooting an elk is shot placement.

FOOTWEAR

As mentioned at the beginning of this chapter, having good boots is important when hunting elk. Elk hunting, and I mean real elk hunting, not hunting from the seat of a pickup or an ATV, invariably involves a good deal of walking and hiking. It also occurs in highly variable weather conditions. Solid footwear is essential. It is difficult to hunt effectively if your feet are wet, cold or blistered.

When I first started elk hunting, I wore a pair of rubber bottom, leather uppers Pac style boots made by Schnee's in Bozeman, MT (the boot is now called the "Hunter II"). I found them to be a great all-round, all weather boot and one that was stout enough to handle all manner of terrain. They are also a very stable boot, good on side slopes and, as I can attest, good for packing out elk quarters. Everyone in our elk camp has a pair. The air bob soles are the best for hunting. Later, I bought a pair of the same style of boot, but more heavily insulated, for colder weather (now called the "Extreme"). Schnee's has unsurpassed customer service and will correct any type of issue without any argument. They also have a rebuild service which will refurbish your boots to near original condition.

In recent years, Schnee's began offering a line of lace up mountain style boots. During a trip to Bozeman a few years ago, I happened to be there during one of their sales and picked up a pair of their Granite boots. These are great boots, insulated, waterproof and excellent in every way. If you like this style of boot, they are an excellent choice.

Another outstanding boot manufacturer is White's Boots in Spokane, WA, a boot company that was founded in 1853. I have a long relationship with White's, dating from my first real job after college when I worked for the U. S. Forest Service in Montana. I worked with engineering field crews and was sometimes involved in firefighting work. When I first started working with the Forest

Service, I had a pair of boots called Herman Survivors. They were billed as the most rugged boot on the planet. Everyone I worked with told me they would not last and that I had better invest in a pair of White's (which everyone else wore). Sure enough, the Survivors did not hold up to our daily forays into the Kootenai National Forest and they slowly fell apart. I ended up making a trip over to Spokane, WA, to get a pair of White's Smokejumper boots. I don't believe you can find a better, more ruggedly constructed boot anywhere. In addition, White's customer service is outstanding in every respect.

Danner Boot Company is another excellent brand. I have a pair of their insulated, waterproof mountain boots and they have worked very well for me elk hunting. They are well made and rugged.

There are other good boot companies out there. What you don't want are the light weight hiking/trail type boots, that are more shoes than a boot. They just won't cut it elk hunting. The bottom line on boots is, like binoculars, get the best that you can afford. You will never be sorry.

CLOTHING AND OTHER GEAR

For some reason, I have always been a fan of wool hunting clothing. This may simply be due to the fact than when I first started hunting deer (in the early 1970's), wool clothing was about all that was available. LL Bean and Woolrich were my go to places in those days. Later, I splurged on a red and black patterned jacket from Filson (I still have it – they last a lifetime.) It was warm and impervious to the weather. In the 1980's, with the development of Gortex, an array of new, synthetic materials began to appear. I tried some of these materials, but mostly found them unsuitable for hunting because they were so noisy. The outstanding features of wool are that it is absolutely quiet in the woods, it does not retain odors, it is very warm and it is very durable. Granted, it is not water proof per se (but a tight weave wool will shed light to moderate rain and snow and will keep you warm even when wet). Paired with a nice, quiet Gortex lined camo rain jacket, you can be comfortable in just about any kind of weather. LL Bean has a couple of excellent rain parkas in the Mossy Oak Country camo pattern. I've used one of these through days of rainy weather hunting whitetail deer in northwest Montana and can vouch for their first class quality. I think the camo pattern is also excellent, a nice mix of black, brown, gray and a bit of green. LL Bean also offers camo wool pants, vests and jackets which are top quality.

Synthetic materials have improved over the years and now there are some pretty good ones out there for hunting. It is often hard to determine if a particular synthetic fabric will be quiet enough though. I have found that running my finger nail across the fabric can give you an indication of how quiet it will be. If it makes even the slightest sound like tearing a sheet of paper, it won't cut it in the field. That means that branches brushing against the garment will make too much noise and will likely alert game. Be sure to check to see what materials have been used in making the garment. If they are composed of acrylic, polyester (aka Elastarell), rayon or similar synthetics, they won't be very quiet. I was looking at some hunting pants a few years ago called Stealth Reaper Extreme Wool manufactured by one of the big outdoor sport clothing companies because they were advertised as "wool hunting pants." When I looked at what they were actually made of, I found that they were composed of only 5% wool, and 95% synthetic materials. The same manufacturer has another pant called the Ridge Reaper Mid Season Wool pant that is composed of 13% wool and 87% acrylic and polyester. These are not true wool pants and I passed on them. They would not have been very quiet in the woods.

I do have some jackets and pants that are made of synthetic materials that are excellent though. A lightweight zip-up jacket made by Kryptek called the Cadog jacket, in their slightly reptilian Highlander camo pattern, is very quiet. It is well designed and warm. I wear it often while elk hunting. It is an excellent light hunting jacket. I believe their other hunting clothing is similarly quiet and well made. Wearing a synthetic material shirt, vest or lightweight jacket as a layer under a wool outer jacket often works well in maintaining a quiet outer clothing layer.

Wool hunting clothing has improved too. Lighter yarns and improved weaving has resulted in some excellent tightly woven, but lightweight clothing that I have found to be really good for hunting. One of the most useful items I have is a wool vest. It is lightweight, compact and very warm. I always take it with me hunting and often put it on under my outer jacket when I am stand hunting. The one I have happens to be from Filson, picked up some years ago during one of their winter sales. It's a terrific garment to have with you while hunting (the "long" model is the best). Filson's clothing is expensive, no question about it, but it will last for as many years as you hunt. They have sales before Christmas, after Christmas and at other times of the year when you can pick up some of their clothing at better prices. Several other manufacturers offer wool vests too, including Woolrich,

Gostwear and Silent Predator. Beretta is another good source of well designed hunting clothing.

In the event you ever need something repaired, the absolute best place for this is Rainy Pass Repairs in Seattle, WA. One year, I left my Kryptek Cadog jacket hanging on a tree next to our elk camp wall tent. When I came back at the end of the day, I found that a pine squirrel had gone to town on it, eating holes all over the back of the jacket (maybe he didn't like the camo pattern or something …). The damage was so bad (it looked like a load of #4 Buckshot had been fired at it), that it was borderline throw away. I was pretty disappointed about this and called Kryptek when I got home and asked about having it repaired. Given the scope of the damage, they referred me to Rainy Pass Repairs. I duly contacted Rainy Pass and spoke with them. They asked that I E-Mail a few photos of the damage, which I did. They got back to me and said to send it up to them and they would see what they could do.

I sent the jacket to them. A few weeks later it was returned to me. The repair was beyond amazing. The jacket looked brand new. Since then, Rainy Pass has repaired a wool gaiter for me and moth damage to a lightweight Filson jacket. They do superlative work. If you ever have a repair need, this is the outfit to contact.

I have noticed in recent years the introduction of quite a few new camouflage patterns aimed at hunters, some of which seem to be inspired by military camo patterns. You probably don't really need the latest special forces camo pattern for elk hunting. What I have found is that the predominant colors in most hunting environments are brown, green, gray and black. As long as the camo you are wearing has that combination of colors, I think you will be in pretty good shape. Choose a pattern that is most suitable for the type of terrain where you hunt. If you are hunting in a desert type environment, a pattern with shades of tan would probably be more appropriate than what you would choose for a conifer forest mountain environment.

Another important item to have is your blaze orange hunting vest (in some states, bright pink can now also be worn). A vest is the way to go here, rather than a solid blaze orange jacket. Where I hunt in Colorado, it can be twenty degrees in the morning and forty-five or even fifty degrees in mid-afternoon. With these wide temperature variances, dressing in layers that can be progressively removed as the day goes on and it gets warmer is the way to go. You can't do this if you have a single blaze orange coat – you are stuck wearing it, regardless of the temperature. With a vest, you have a lot more flexibility with regard to what you wear, regardless of weather conditions. There have been some years when it has been unseasonably warm during elk season and I have worn my vest over a wool shirt. Other years, when it has been in the teens or single digits, I have worn it over a wool parka.

The best vest out there used to be made by Filson. The vest was originally designed for surveryors, engineers, geologists and other technical people who work in the field. Unfortunately, with Filson's shift away from hunting over the past ten or so years, the vest is no longer available. The best vest available now is the Pro 10-Pocket Cruiser Vest (#94581) made by JIM-GEM. LL Bean also has a good, basic type hunting vest and another good vest is the Terra-Tech 10-Pocket Cruiser vest.

Hunting packs are also an important item. There are dozens of various types of packs on the market and I think the one that works best for you is largely a matter of personal choice. In our elk camp, with four hunters, there are four different types of packs. After having used probably half a dozen different styles of packs over the years, the one that I found that I like best is a lumbar style (shoulder straps with a padded waist band) made by Nimrod Outdoor Company. The design of this pack originated with the military and is widely used by wildland firefighters. (I was issued an early version of it, probably military surplus, when I fought fires on a Forest Service fire crew in the mid-1970's.) You can carry a lot of gear in and on the Nimrod pack. The one I use is their Pinnacle model. The thing I like most about it is how it distributes weight to your waist and hips so that there is not so much weight on your shoulders. I can comfortably carry twenty-five or thirty pounds of gear all day. There are lots of pockets, interior and exterior, for hunting items ranging from flashlights, headlamps, water bottles, extra batteries, first aid kit – you name it. Straps on the outside can be used to attach extra clothing. They come in different sizes with varying capacities and you can get them lined or unlined with Gortex. This pack has always worked very well for me. (I use one for deer hunting too.)

Always have a first aid kit with you. I don't mean one of the little trail first aid kits in a zip pouch you pick up at REI, I mean one that you put together yourself. I have cut myself several times over the years while dressing out or skinning elk, one time pretty seriously. You should have some large Band-Aids, gauze pads, rolled gauze, Quick Clot gauze and Co-Lastic wrap (aka Vet Wrap) to treat any minor "wounds" you incur in the process of dressing and/or skinning an elk. Another essential item is a tourniquet for a really dire wound. The best ones are called CAT Tourniquets and can be obtained from numerous sources online. Always have it with you. (I speak from personal experience on this point – more about it later.)

Always have two knives. Sharpen them *before* you go hunting and be sure to have a small knife sharpener with you when you hunt. I have never been able to dress out, skin and quarter an elk with only one knife. Having the second knife allows you to work more effectively and efficiently, without having to constantly sharpen your knife as you go. You will also need a saw for quartering your elk. (This assumes you are not going the boning out route.) One of the best that I have used is the Wyoming Saw made by the Wyoming Knife Company. The thing that makes this saw so good is that you can use a real butcher's bone blade with it and it has a real handle that you can get your hand around and grip. I have tried, and jettisoned, a couple of the lighter duty, curved handle type of saws. They just don't cut it and I would not waste your money on them.

Dress out your elk as promptly as possible after shooting it. For the best meat quality, it is critically important to cool the meat as quickly as you can. After dressing out the animal, skin it immediately to release the animal's body heat from the carcass. Leaving the hide on will result in poor quality meat. After dressing out and skinning, start quartering the carcass (or boning out the meat). We always put the quarters in cotton mesh game bags to protect them from leaves, pine needles, dirt and any other forest debris. It takes me a solid three to four hours to dress out, skin and quarter an elk. It is a lot of work and you will need to take your time doing it. Once you have your elk quarters back in camp, be sure to place them in a shady spot, out of direct sunlight. Even if you put the meat in coolers, they need to be in the shade. Below our camp on Mountain B, there is a shallow draw in a thick, little conifer stand that we call the "cold spot." We noticed over the years that that the snow always remained in this area the longest. We found that the combination of the draw, the heavy timber shading and the fact that the sun just did not shine on this spot very long during the day, resulted in it staying a good ten degrees cooler than just about anyplace else. We began "storing" our elk quarters there, using it as a sort of meat locker until we packed up our camp.

I am a big believer in redundancy. I carry two of almost everything – two flashlights (Streamlight Scorpions), two knives, extra batteries for the flashlights and a headlamp, extra bulbs for the flashlights, plus a compass. The Scorpion flashlight is excellent and I have used them for many years, but there are many other great flashlights out there now of a similar compact size, brightness, durability and battery longevity. Get what you like the best. I also carry a small stash of survival gear in the event I have to spend the night in the woods or wait for a rescue. Essential items include a Mylar survival blanket, some food (thin foil packages of tuna and Spam), waterproof matches and a magnesium fire starter stick, plus some tinder to help get a fire started. I also have a small strobe light (and extra batteries, of course) in case I have to mark my location at night.

As I mentioned in the Introduction, I have packed out, on foot, every elk I have ever shot, around 140 quarters of elk. Each quarter averaged 75-85 pounds and it goes without saying, that it is a real workout, particularly where we hunt, where every step you take is uphill to get back to camp at the top of Mountain B. This is where all that physical conditioning preparation really pays off. In order to do this, you have to have a decent pack frame, one designed for packing heavy loads.

The best one out there is made by Bull Pacs of Vancouver, WA. The story I originally heard about Bull Pacs was that the guy who founded the company (originally in Idaho) was an avid elk hunter.

He could not find a decent pack frame on the market to pack out elk quarters. He had some welding skills, so he started experimenting with various heavy load pack designs. After developing several prototype models, the Bull Pacs pack frame was born. In contrast to the four different styles of hunting gear packs in our elk camp, there are four Bull Pacs pack frames. I have packed out the vast majority of my elk quarters with one, plus a few quarters for my hunting companions. The Bull Pacs pack frame is the one I have used for years and can recommend unequivocally (note though, that Nimrod also makes a similar design pack frame).

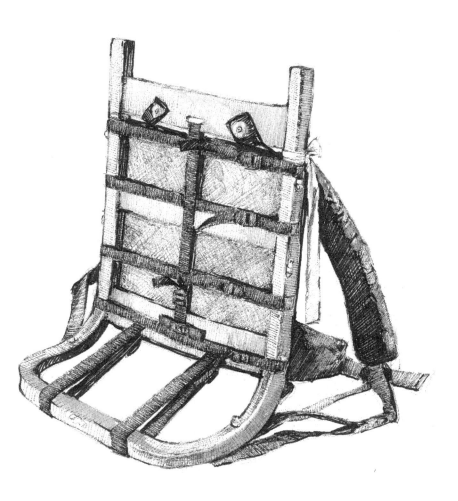

CHAPTER 4

ELK HUNTING TACTICS AND TECHNIQUES

How you hunt elk depends on a number of factors. At the top of the list is the type of terrain where you hunt, what I call your "hunting environment." Other factors include how well you know your hunting area, your physical condition, your motivation for hunting and how you like to hunt. Some hunters don't like sitting on a stand, waiting for an animal to come by, they want to be moving, searching for animals. Other hunters are fine sitting on a stand. These are the types of things that will shape your hunting style and the techniques you use to hunt.

While most elk in the western States are found in mountainous country, not all are. Elk are a highly adaptable animal and can survive in varied climates and environments and on varied food sources (much like whitetail deer).

As mentioned earlier, some elk here in Colorado are found in plains environments. Fred and I once hunted in a plains area east of Walsenburg, CO, probably forty miles from the nearest mountain. It is pretty wide open country, but also has some relief, lots of rocky outcrops, draws and lots of thick juniper stands. You could certainly be presented with a long shot situation here, but you could also be presented with a twenty-five yard shot. It is a semi-arid environment and water is a big factor for game. Surprisingly, there are some pretty large elk herds in the area. We did not know the area at all and spent almost all of our time roaming around trying to find the elk. We never did find them.

Some elk in Colorado spend all of their time during the summer and fall high in the mountains above tree line (generally above 11,000 -12,000 feet in Colorado). I have a friend who likes to hunt up high in the various Colorado mountain ranges. He spends most of his time on high, rocky ridges glassing for animals on other ridges, down in valleys and on benches in between. Not being a fan of ultra long range shots, if he spots some animals he then tries to maneuver, using whatever rocky cover is available, into a position from which he can have a shot. He's pretty good at 300 - 400 yard shots and he told me once that he made one shot at just under 500 yards. He practices shooting at these ranges a lot and is very good at it. In 2017, he shot a huge 7x8 bull in a large treeless bowl near Weston Pass, southwest of Fairplay, CO. It is not my kind of hunting, but he sure loves it.

Elk are also present in semi-desert environments in New Mexico, Arizona, Utah and Nevada. Your style of hunting there will likely be a lot different than the way Fred and I hunt on Mountains A, B and C. I have a friend in Montana who has hunted several times in the Missouri Breaks area in the eastern side of the state, near the Fort Peck Reservoir. There are no mountains within a hundred miles of that location, but a robust population of elk inhabit the brushy draws that lead down to the reservoir. He tells me it is tough hunting due to the rugged, deep draws that are full of dense cover. He and his hunting partner often walk the low ridges on either side of a draw, one on either side, glassing down into the draw. Other times, one of them will get down into the draw and fight their way through the juniper and oak brush while the other hunter walks above, ready to shoot if any animals move out of the cover. They tailor their hunting style to their hunting environment.

Since most elk are found in mountainous areas, similar to where Fred and I hunt, I will focus on that type of elk hunting environment. As discussed in chapter 1, our hunting style underwent an evolution over the years at Mountain A, B and C. Initially, we roamed far and wide, searching for animals and trying to have an opportunity for a shot. As we learned the area, we started spending more time on stands, having animals come to us through their natural movements and also letting other hunters do some of the legwork for us in moving animals our way. Over time, we found areas where we could usually count on seeing animals. I think you need to exercise some flexibility in how you hunt, depending on the conditions in your area. If you hunt in a place where there are lots of other hunters, taking a stand might be a good approach, letting the other hunters move the animals around. Where Fred and I hunt, there are not so many other hunters around that we could take that approach, so we combine some stand hunting with some walking and checking out pockets of cover that sometimes contain animals.

Some snow, up to five or six inches, can be a huge aid in

trying to locate animals. It makes them easier to spot against the white background and it allows for tracking, which can be a very successful way to find animals. In chapter 2, I related my experience with the bedded bull in the aspen grove, which resulted from my finding the tracks of that band of elk. A few years later, I had another experience tracking an elk. It had snowed about four inches one night, so first thing in the morning I headed out, looking to cut some elk tracks. I began at the base of Mountain B and roamed around the lower finger ridges there without finding any. The weather was clear and sunny that day and it warmed up quickly. Around 11 AM, I decided that some animals might be higher up on Mountain B, perhaps bedded down soaking up the warm sun, so I slowly hunted my way uphill. While I was carefully making my way along the steep south facing side of Mountain B, constantly glassing ahead, I spotted an elk, comfortably bedded down next to a fallen lodgepole pine, about seventy-five yards away. He had spotted me and a staring contest ensued, with me trying to determine if he was a legal bull, and he probably trying to assess how much of a risk I was to him. He slowly got up off his bed and I saw that he was a good five point bull. I was in the process of bringing up my rifle when he took off, angling uphill away from me. I took off after him, moving as fast as I could, sometimes running, following his trail in the snow. It went twisting and turning for about half a mile, up to the top of Mountain B. I had not spent much time on top of Mountain B at that time, so I was in unfamiliar territory. I doggedly stayed on his trail as it weaved between large pine and spruce trees. Then, I came around one tree and there he was, broadside to me, looking straight at me, forty yards away. I knew he was only a second or two away from bolting. I threw my rifle to my shoulder, aimed just behind his shoulder and fired, all in one fluid motion. He dropped right to the ground – I had hit him straight through the heart.

Just to show you that this tracking technique does not work all the time, another year, in the same general area, I was again hunting slowly across the south flank of Mountain B. There was a good twelve or fourteen inches of snow on the ground and it was heavy going. I reached a place where the aspen trees transitioned into conifers. I was heading uphill, approaching the top area of Mountain B when I spotted a bull getting up off his bed, about sixty yards above me. Before I could do anything, he wheeled around and disappeared. I hiked up to his bedding spot as quickly as I could and took off after him. This bull led me on a torturous path through the densest cover on top of Mountain B. As I followed his trail, I came upon places where I could tell he had stopped and looked back to see if I was still coming. I could never spot him though. I pushed and pushed for several hours, hoping to get sight of him again. A couple of times, I found spots where he had bedded down and rested, so I knew I was pushing him hard. I followed him through the heavy snow for several miles. He went down steep draws and up the other sides, always remaining out of sight. Finally, at the bottom of one deep draw, his tracks merged with those of a group of eight or ten other elk. I followed the group of tracks for a few hundred yards but finally realized that I had lost his track and that there was no way to determine where he had gone. He had won that contest (besides, I was pretty beat at that point), so I turned and slowly made my way back to camp, some three miles distant.

One of the other major factors that influences how you hunt is your physical condition. You are not going to be able to track and chase an elk in a high altitude environment, like the two examples above, unless you have spent some time preparing for it. If you are not in good physical condition, you will likely be limited to where and how much you can hunt. Stand hunting may be your most realistic option. Another option is what I call a "stalk and stop" type hunting style where you hunt slowly along (glassing ahead, of course), stop and sit for fifteen or twenty minutes, then move on another few hundred yards, stop again and so on. This can be a very effective way to hunt.

At the time of year that Fred and I usually hunt, the elk rut is largely over, so elk bugling has ended or is greatly diminished. Almost every year though, it seems that there is still a bull or two out there that bugles occasionally. Hearing a bugle is similar to a neon sign lighting up. Now you know with specificity where the bull is located and you can go after him. Always be extra careful on your approach to a bugling bull, as he will be with a number of cows and it is easy to be detected by them. Even if you have gotten serious about controlling your scent, always approach from the downwind direction. Spend more time glassing ahead than moving. Crawl if you need to. If those cows, or the bull, spot you (they don't have to scent you), they will likely bolt and you will not have a shot. This is yet another reason to be in good physical condition. Imagine how frustrating it would be to hear a bull bugling some distance away but feel that you can't take advantage of the opportunity because you aren't physically up to hiking over to where he is located.

I don't mean to hammer on the physical conditioning aspect of elk hunting too much, but the fact is that it is really important and can have a real impact on your hunting style and technique. One time, Fred and I encountered a group of hunters on top of Mountain B, near our camp, who stopped us for a conversation.

They were most interested in learning where we hunted. When we gave them our stock answer, an ambiguous "down below," they commented that they could not possibly hunt down there because they could not handle hiking the steep slopes. That's fine, because you certainly have to recognize your limitations, which this group of hunters did. For them though, it clearly limited where they could hunt and reduced their chances for finding animals.

Another aspect related to this concerns how you are going to get your animal out in the event you shoot one. I have found that elk quarters weigh 75-85 pounds on average. On a really big bull, they will weigh more. One of the limiting factors where we hunt is the packing distance from camp. Some of the terrain is so steep and so far from camp that it simply is not realistic to hunt there from a packing out standpoint.

One alternative to quartering your elk is boning it out, basically carving all the useable meat off the bones of the elk and packing out just the meat. This can lighten your packing load for sure. If you have even a passable skill at carving with a knife, this may be a viable option for you (I have never done it). Be sure to have two knives and a sharpener.

The point here is that you need to think realistically about what you can handle from a physical standpoint when it comes to packing and then tailor your hunting style and strategy to your physical abilities. The last thing you want is to get too aggressive and get into a jam physically on the side of some mountain at 10,000 feet. Be prepared – get into shape.

Depending on where you hunt and how well you know your hunting area, I think combining stand hunting with walking (technically referred to as "still hunting") is a good way to hunt elk. Even if you do not know your area that well, the walking part helps you learn your area. If there is snow on the ground and you cut a track or a group of tracks, you can then follow them and try to close on the animals. In dry powdery snow, I find it impossible to tell how old tracks are, but in wetter snow, you can sometimes get a feel for whether they are fresh or old by running your finger across the track impression to see if the surface is soft or hard. I have always found that a softer surface suggests a fresher track.

Occasionally, other hunters set up a camp near where we have our camp. One year, a couple of guys pitched a small tent at the beginning of the route that Fred and I take to go to our respective hunting spots. Opening morning, we got up at our usual 4:45AM or so and left camp at about 6AM to be on our stands by 6:45AM, about fifteen minutes before it began to get light. We walked right past the tent of these two hunters and were amazed to find that they were still fast asleep. I could not believe it. On opening morning (or any morning you hunt), you want to be at the top of your game, in position and ready to go before it begins to get light.

I believe that in order to hunt effectively and be successful, you need to hunt all day, from before dawn to last shooting light. We have always hunted that way. Had I not gotten to my stand early enough to be there when that big six point bull came by, I would have missed that opportunity. If you are headed to a stand location, get there in the dark and get settled and organized so you don't have to do this later when animals could be approaching. The last thing you want is to lose a shot opportunity because you are fumbling around in your pack looking for something and get spotted by some animals that have approached you unseen and unheard. Minimize your movements on a stand. Always assume that animals have your location under observation as they approach. If you are busy moving around, they will probably spook or move away, resulting in losing a potential opportunity for a shot.

Another good thing to do is get your binoculars focused and your riflescope adjusted to an appropriate setting for your location. Just about every year, I hear of hunters that missed a shot opportunity because they had not dialed their scope power down to a lower level when they entered a section of heavy timber and then wasted precious seconds doing this when they saw an elk. If you have caps on your scope and they don't need to be closed over your ocular and objectives lenses, open them so you don't need to do this if you see an animal. Time is of the essence when you have an opportunity for a shot. You don't want to be distracted focusing your binoculars, adjusting your scope or doing anything else. You want to be focused with laser intensity on making the shot.

I am always amazed when we drive past other camps, usually on our way out after a successful hunt, how many hunters are lounging around their camps at mid-day, sitting in chairs, stoking a campfire or just standing around. I can never figure out why they are not out hunting. After all, it's not likely that they are going to see an elk while hanging around in camp.

Perseverance is another key success factor in elk hunting. Elk are really good at disappearing after the shooting starts on opening day, quickly retreating to secure areas where hunters are less likely to find them. I have shot elk at literally every hour of daylight, from first light (like that big six point bull) all through the morning and all through the afternoon, right up to just before dark. If you head back to camp after just a few hours of morning hunting and hang around there till later in the day before wandering out again, you are really shortchanging yourself. If you are serious about elk hunting, and by that, I mean you really want to go home with an animal, you have to have the perseverance to be out in the woods, hunting, all day, dark to dark. If you don't do this, you commensurately reduce your chances of finding an elk and having an opportunity for a shot. If nothing else, think about all the effort you have gone to to go elk hunting, getting organized and prepared, traveling to your hunting location, setting up camp and everything else involved. Why wouldn't you spend every available minute hunting ?

To be fair, people go hunting for a variety of reasons. Some people really want to get an animal and will hunt long and hard to find one. For others, going hunting is a chance to get away from their day to day grind and spend some time away in unspoiled country with some friends. Some people are more casual about hunting. They wander around in the morning a little bit, sit for a while, head back to camp for lunch and maybe go back out later in the day if they feel like it. If they run into an animal and have a shot, fine and if they don't, that's fine too. If that's what you want to do, that's entirely OK. One guy I know is the cook at his elk camp and that's all does, preparing breakfast, packing lunches and making dinner for the other guys in camp. He never goes out hunting. This is what he enjoys doing and if someone does shoot an elk, they always share the bounty with him. This is how he likes to spend his time "hunting" and there is nothing wrong with that.

A couple of other suggestions regarding hunting techniques are in order before wrapping up this chapter. I described the practice of glassing ahead in chapter 2. I won't go into again here, but if you want to be a successful elk hunter, there is, in my opinion, no other single hunting technique that will contribute more to your success than glassing ahead as you hunt. Glassing ahead allows you to spot animals earlier than you otherwise would have, thereby allowing you to get into position to have a shot. I will relate one more experience to hammer home the importance and value of glassing ahead.

This particular situation occurred this past year (2019). It was the second day of the season. Some cows had walked by me twenty yards away on opening day, but I had not seen any bulls (I only had a bull tag). There was about fifteen inches of dry, powdery snow on the ground. It had been a slow day and after spending a couple of hours on the afternoon stand over the mid-day hours, at about 2:30 PM, I decided to set out and look for some elk tracks.

About two hundred yards west of the afternoon stand, I found a single set of tracks coming up from the bottom of Mountain B, headed uphill into the thick timber along the west side of the mountain. There was no way to tell if the tracks were fresh or whether they had been made many hours before, but I neverthe-less decided to follow them, glassing ahead periodically.

After about five hundred yards, I approached the transition from the steep slope of Mountain B to the flatter top area. I paused to glass ahead and as I did, I saw an elk rising up off its bed about thirty yards uphill from me. The elk was getting up hind end first and all I could see was its back half. Its front half was obscured by several lodgepole pine tree trunks.

My binoculars were in my hand and I immediately brought them up to determine if the elk was a legal bull for me (four point minimum). As I did so, the elk raised up on its front legs and I saw a large set of antlers come up off the ground behind the trees.

I instantly brought my rifle up, but even before I had it fully to my shoulder (arm movement !!), the bull spun around and bolted away downhill, disappearing in a second or two.

I went after him. He raced down through the timber into the deep draw between Mountain B and Mountain C and kept right on going up the slope through the thick stand of aspens on the east side of Mountain C. He easily outpaced me and was nowhere to be seen when I started climbing the steep sixty-degree slope of Mountain C.

I doggedly stayed on his trail and followed him for a couple of miles, without ever spotting him. With only an hour or so of daylight remaining, I reluctantly broke off the chase and headed back to camp.

I made two fundamental mistakes here. First, I did not really expect to run into an elk after following the tracks for only about five hundred yards and I was surprised when I saw the bull rising from his bed. Second, because I did not expect to encounter an elk so soon after beginning to follow the tracks, I was bit lax in my glassing ahead. Had I glassed ahead more diligently, I believe that I would have spotted this bull fifty or sixty yards away and would probably have been able to maneuver into a position to have had a shot at him on his bed.

What made this experience particularly painful was that in all of my years of hunting elk, I have never walked up to within thirty yards of a bedded bull. I don't know if the bull was in deep slumber, if he could not see me approaching due to the tree trunks near his head or whether perhaps he had some sort of injury to his right eye (the one that was facing me). None of that really matters. What matters is that I thoroughly blew this opportunity.

The lessons here are if you decide to follow an elk track, assume the tracks are smoking fresh and that you may encounter the animal at any time. There is no point in following tracks if you do not have that mindset. Glass ahead frequently, every ten or fifteen yards. Do not make the mistakes I made here by not expecting to run into the elk so soon and not glassing ahead frequently enough. These mistakes almost certainly cost me a solid shot at this bull.

Another useful technique, similar to glassing ahead, is what I call "scanning." The difference between glassing ahead and scanning is that when you are glassing ahead you are moving and when you are simply scanning, you are not moving. Scanning is helpful when you are on a stand or when you have paused while still hunting (walking or "stalk and stop" type hunting) for one reason or another. It means that you take a quick look around, with or without your binoculars, to make sure that no animals have approached unseen or unheard before you get going again. This is an important thing to do given the ability of elk to move through terrain in complete silence and appear from unexpected directions. If you are hunting on a stand, be sure to scan in all directions periodically. Remember that elk sometimes move with the wind, so don't fix your attention on just one direction from which you expect animals to appear. When still hunting, if you sit down to rest, have lunch or pause for some other reason, always take a quick look around before getting back up. You never know when some elk might appear behind you or off to the side. Scanning is one more little skill that can make a difference when elk hunting. The following examples demonstrate why it is worth doing.

One year, I stopped on the side of a timbered nose for lunch. I spent about an hour there and then got slowly up and shouldered my pack. I picked up my rifle, turned and looked up toward the top of the nose, about fifty yards away. I was stunned to see a big bull standing there looking right at me. He had come up the nose from down below. As soon as he realized that I had seen him, he spun around and bolted back down the nose.

Naturally, I went after him. There was about two inches of snow on the ground, just enough to hold a track. I followed him down into the deep draw between Mountain B and Mountain C and then through the aspens up the steep side of Mountain C. About halfway up, his tracks headed onto a long bench feature along the south side of Mountain C. I followed the tracks through the aspens when all of a sudden, I spotted him about seventy-five yards ahead of me. He was facing dead away from me, standing at a slight angle with his head and neck turned back looking at me. I raised my rifle, trying to determine if I had a shot or not. I had a clear line of fire, and I felt confident about taking a neck shot, so after a few more seconds to get settled, I fired. The bull took off and disappeared into a patch of pine and spruce trees ahead of him. I ran up to where he had been standing and looked for evidence of a hit, but could find nothing. I continued to follow him and eventually determined that I had missed. I followed him another half mile or so, as he led me through a jungle of thick blowdowns and dense conifer stands. I finally realized that this animal had the upper hand in this situation and that after being shot at once, he was not going to give me another opportunity. I admitted defeat and headed back over to Mountain B.

This was my scanning lesson. Had I been a little more on the ball at my lunch spot and taken just a few seconds to turn around and scan behind me before getting up, I probably would have shot that bull from where I had been sitting. I took this lesson to heart and adopted scanning as one of my standard operating procedures from that point on.

It paid off a few years later when I was hunting off my tree stand one opening morning. A light breeze was blowing from the west, so I was positioned sitting, facing east, the direction from which I most expected any animals to approach. At about 9 AM or so, I heard some commotion behind me, off to the west. I turned around, thinking it might be some elk coming down from above, but it turned out to be three or four mule deer, evidently spooked by some hunter further upslope. As was my habit now, I did a quick scan off to the west and uphill. As I glassed past one group of aspen trees about eighty yards away with my binoculars, I noted a little patch of tan color that seemed slightly different than the rest of the tall, tan colored grass among the aspens. I continued my scan and when I was finished, I returned to that little tan patch of color. I stared at it for several minutes, until I finally realized that what I was looking at was the light tan coat on the mid section of an elk. Aspen trees obscured both the front and the back of the animal. I quickly got my rifle in my right hand and continued to stare at the animal through my binoculars, trying to determine if it was a bull or a cow. Finally, the elk took a step forward and stood there looking in my direction. It was a smallish five-point bull, yet another animal that was traveling with the wind behind him. The problem was he had already spotted me, probably when I had swiveled around to look at the deer, and he was on full alert. In addition, I did not have a shot because his heart/lung area and his neck were still obscured by aspen tree trunks. He acted very nervous and I was really concerned that he would wheel around and take off back to the west. Instead, he began moving at a fast trot diagonally uphill through the aspens. This was a bad situation from a shooting perspective because there was no chance for a shot while he was moving so fast through the trees, seventy-five to eighty yards away. He reached a trail that went on contour through the aspens above me. I searched for a clear lane up through the trees and found one about four feet wide that I knew he would have to pass through as he moved across the slope. I decided I would shoot as soon as he entered the lane. I got set to shoot, sitting in a rock solid position, watching him trot through the trees along the trail. He entered the open lane and, incredibly, stopped. He stood there looking down the slope at me. I had a perfect broadside shot and I fired.

Had I not scanned after seeing those deer come down to the west of me, I doubt I that I would have seen this bull. Despite my previous experience with animals moving with the wind behind them, I was still expecting to see any elk approach from the east, moving into the wind, so I was looking mostly eastward. Had I managed to spot this bull without having seen him when I did, it probably would have been too late, as he was moving diagonally uphill, and would likely have been so obscured by the aspens uphill that there would not have been an opportunity for a shot. Overall, I consider myself fortunate to have taken this animal, which I attribute to my having learned my scanning lesson well. Make scanning a habit. It's another little skill that can make the difference between a successful hunt and an unsuccessful one.

One more suggestion concerns keeping your eyes on an elk if you spot one. One year I was hunting down below Mountain A, moving slowly along through the aspens and conifer stands, glassing ahead, looking for some animals. It was about mid-day and I approached a small clearing in a flat area among the trees. As I glassed ahead into the aspens on the far side of the clearing, I was amazed to see a nice, big bull walking along through the trees just inside the far edge of the clearing, about seventy-five yards away.

I was thirty yards from the edge of the clearing and I was concerned that if I approached any further, the bull would spot me. There was a small knoll off to my left and I decided that if I could move around it, using it to screen my movement from the bull, I would be in a good position to have a shot at the bull when he came into view from behind the knoll (in making this move, I was assuming the bull would continue on the same course he was on when I first saw him).

I moved around my side of the little knoll, found a good shooting position and waited for the bull. He never appeared. After about ten minutes, hoping that the bull had paused in or on the edge of the clearing, I crept around the knoll to a point where I had a good view of the clearing and the trees on the other side. He was nowhere to be seen. He had apparently either spotted me and moved off or had simply taken a turn on his own and drifted out of sight off into the aspens.

The lesson here is to never take your eyes off your target. There is no way to know where an animal will go once you lose sight of it and assuming it will continue on a given course is a risky assumption, as I learned. In retrospect, I should have gotten down on my hands and knees as soon as I spotted the bull and crawled to the edge of the clearing to try to have a shot at him from there, keeping him in view the entire time. I never made this mistake again.

I mentioned it in the previous chapter, but it is important enough to mention again. Always remember that your first shot is your best shot. Hopefully, the animal will not be aware of your presence and you will have time to carefully set up your shot so as to achieve solid shot placement in a vital area on the animal. This will be your best opportunity. After you fire, the animal will likely be moving, which will probably present a more difficult shooting situation, even if it is in an open area. If you are in a timbered area, your first shot may well be your only shot. Make it your best.

I hope you have realized by now that in order to hunt elk effectively and successfully you need to do more than one or two things right, you need to do a lot of things right all together. You need to be well equipped and you need to be able to shoot accurately. You need to have the judgement to know when you have a shot and when you don't. You need to control your scent and at the same time be mindful of wind currents in the event your scent control is not 100% effective. You need to be in decent physical shape. You need to have perseverance. Little details like having your binoculars and rifle scope focused properly for the terrain in which you are hunting matter. You need to glass ahead when moving and to scan when you are not moving. You need to be very careful with your arm movement when elk are in view. You need to remember that your first shot is your best shot and you need to always remember that shot placement is the most important thing in shooting an elk. And of course, you need a little bit of luck too.

Finally, if you spend any time in stands of heavy timber, it will not take long before you are harassed by those often highly annoying little denizens of the forest, pine squirrels. These pesky little creatures are very territorial and really resent trespassers entering into their little pine squirrel kingdoms. I have had some sit in a pine or spruce tree above me and chatter away for fifteen or twenty minutes at a time. They can be a real pain.

Ironically, they can, occasionally, help you. More than once I have heard a pine squirrel start squeaking and chattering down below me in heavy timber and then have elk come into view. They resent the intrusion from elk just as they resent it from you. This does not happen very often, but I have had it happen often enough that if a pine squirrel starts making a lot of noise for no apparent reason, I pay attention to it and bring my binoculars up. You never know what might appear, maybe nothing, maybe some elk.

CHAPTER 5

HUNTING
ETHICS

A peculiar virtue in wildlife ethics is that the hunter
ordinarily has no gallery to applaud or disapprove
of his conduct. Whatever his acts, they are dictated by
his own conscience, rather than that of onlookers.
It is difficult to exaggerate the importance of this fact.

—Aldo Leopold

Hunting in an ethical manner is a big deal to me, and it should be a big deal to everyone who ventures out in pursuit of game. Ethical hunting involves many factors that on a combined basis, result in hunters not having an overwhelming advantage over the game they are hunting. It involves having the judgment to know when to shoot and when not to shoot. It also involves a profound respect for the animal you are hunting and an obligation that if you take an animal's life, it will be done in a clean, quick manner with minimal suffering to the animal.

The most fundamental aspect of minimizing suffering to the animal means that you have sufficient knowledge of the animal's physiology to know where to shoot it to achieve as quick a kill as possible. It also means that you have taken the time to practice with your weapon and know enough about your weapon (and your ammunition), that you know with confidence that you can hit your target in a vital place.

I believe that my definition of "having a shot" is an integral part of ethical hunting. You know by now that in order to have a shot, you must first have a clear line of fire to your target. This means no trees or other obstructions that might deflect the bullet you fire. If you hunt in mountainous terrain where there are thick stands of conifer and aspen trees, in almost all cases this precludes taking a shot at a running animal. It also precludes any type of "snap" shots. It clearly precludes just "taking a shot" at an animal, a situation where you don't really know where your bullet may hit the animal or even if it will. Second, you must be confident that the bullet you fire will hit the animal in a vital area which will result in a quick kill and a minimum of suffering. This also precludes just "taking a shot" because you don't know if you can place your bullet in a vital area on the animal. It preludes taking shots at animals running through timber, it precludes "snap" shots and taking "dead astern" shots. As discussed in the section about elk rifles in chapter 3, don't take a long range shot if you are not skilled at long range shooting (most hunters are not). Under those circumstances you do not have a shot. When you simply "take a shot," all you are doing is firing a shot at the animal, without any confidence that you can actually place your bullet in a vital area on the animal. This can, and does, result in many wounded animals. This is unethical hunting.

One year, around 11 AM, I was hunting just below the crest of a ridge below Mountain B. I was moving slowly through a grove of aspens when I spotted a large bull moving along the ridgetop, about fifty yards above me, headed in my direction. I stopped and watched him move along, closing the range. When he was at point almost directly above me and in an open lane through the trees, I aimed for his heart area, fired and he dropped to the ground. He was a really nice five by six-point bull with heavy beamed, mahogany colored antlers. I dressed him out and began skinning him. As I removed the hide, I was astounded to find a number of bullet wounds on him, four in all, other than my shot to his heart. One hit was high on his shoulder, another in his hind quarter, a grazing hit on his stomach just in front of his hind legs and he was gut shot. About two hours later, as I was finishing up quartering him, a hunter approached from the general direction of the bull's backtrail. He came up and told me that this was his bull, that he and his friend had shot it down in the timber on the north side of the ridge that morning. He seemed to think that I had found it lying dead on the ground. I told him what had happened, that the bull was moving along just fine and that I did not discover he had been shot until I skinned him out. The guy wanted to argue about this, first wanting half the meat, then wanting the head and antlers. (I was considering suggesting that he work on his marksmanship, but I thought that it would probably not be a constructive comment, under the circumstances.) I was concerned that a real problem was going to develop, but when he realized that he wasn't getting anywhere with me, he wandered off.

What happened here, of course, is that this hunter and his friend had jumped this bull in the heavy timber on the north side of the ridge and had simply opened up on it, shooting wildly, hoping for a hit. This is a prime example of just "taking a shot," versus "having a shot." This is reckless, irresponsible and unethical (and unfortunately, all too common). This bull would undoubtedly have died, probably in some tangled patch of blowdowns, never to be found except by the ravens, coyotes and bears. I have always believed that the hunting gods had somehow arranged for my path and the bull's to converge, so that this was not the outcome for this fine animal.

Another year, I was hunting near the deep draw between Mountain A and Mountain B. Late in the morning, I heard a bull bugling from a stand of heavy timber on a nose below Mountain A. Even though it was right on the margin of being too far from camp to realistically hunt, I nevertheless headed down there to see if I could find the elk. I hiked up to the top of a high point on the nose and slowly made my way down, with the uphill thermal flow coming toward me. I had to pass through a stand of aspens before reaching the conifer stand where the elk were. While I slowly made my way through the aspen grove, the bull below bugled a couple more times. It sounded like he was at the top of a teardrop formation of elk in the timber. I was already beginning to think about how I was going to pack him out. I reached the edge of the conifers and began glassing down through the trees. All I saw were white wapiti rumps trotting away through the timber. I had been spotted out in the aspens, and the elk were not hanging around. They headed further down the nose, way too far from camp for me to pursue them.

I turned and headed back toward Mountain A. As I entered another large stand of aspens, I came upon a well used game trail. All the aspen leaves were on the ground and the trail looked like a gold ribbon snaking down through the trees. Since it headed in the same general direction that I was headed, I decided to follow it. I came to a spot where the trail went around a large rock outcrop, about thirty feet high. I walked slowly around the outcrop and came face to face with a big bull, coming up the trail, less than ten yards away. We stared at each other for a second or two and then he bolted, diving off the trail, headed downhill. I threw my rifle up but almost immediately realized I had no shot. The bull was bobbing and weaving through the trees, jumping over blowdowns and ducking under others as he accelerated away. I watched him go and in four or five seconds, he was out of sight.

I have often thought about this bull, because many hunters would have taken a shot (or two) at him. It would not have been the right thing to do though, as the probability of hitting him in a vital spot was almost nonexistent and the probability of wounding him, if you did hit him, was high. It would have been unethical to have fired. A big part of being an ethical hunter is having the judgment to know when to shoot and when not to shoot. That was a situation where it would not have been right to shoot.

Also, be mindful of not hitting more than one animal when making your shot. This can easily happen when another elk is standing behind the one you are targeting. If your bullet is properly placed in the heart/lung zone, it will likely pass through the elk you are shooting at. If another animal is standing behind it, in the line of fire, it will also be hit [this comes up in the next chapter, Firearms/ Hunting Safety, in the form of the fourth basic firearms safety rule: Always be certain of your target and beyond].

I have experienced this situation numerous times and on occasion have had to pass on taking a shot due to the risk of hitting another animal. One time, I ran into about a dozen elk approaching through a stand of aspen trees on contour about thirty yards upslope from me. I saw them first and they were unaware of my presence. The group was comprised of cows, a spike bull and two smallish five point bulls. For some reason, as they approached, the two five point bulls peeled off from the group, headed downhill and then stopped, broadside to me, about forty yards away. The problem was that they were standing exactly next to each other. It was clear that if I fired at one bull, my shot would pass through and also hit the second bull. I waited patiently for one of the bulls to move off so that I could safely shoot. Suddenly, one of them sprang into a fast trot, headed downhill. Just as I was preparing to squeeze the trigger on the remaining bull, he took off after the first one, racing down through the aspen trees, seemingly trying to catch up with him. It was a lost opportunity, but not one that I regretted, as there was no shot to be had in this situation. I was not going to kill two bulls to take just one.

Another cornerstone of ethical hunting is what is referred to as "Fair Chase." Fair chase in its broadest context is hunting using lawful and socially acceptable methods to pursue and take game. Running game down with vehicles, ATV's, snowmobiles, aircraft and other machines is not fair chase. Employing other forms of technology, like drones, to locate and/or move animals in a desired direction is not fair chase. I have always considered devices like hearing amplifiers and similar hunting gadgets, as well as practices like using networks of game cameras to "pattern" game movements to be entirely inconsistent with fair chase hunting because they tilt the playing field in the hunter's favor at the expense of the animal. Don't use equipment that gives you an unfair advantage. Always hunt according to the principles of fair chase.

Following game laws is an important part of ethical hunting and fair chase. These laws are in place to protect game and game populations, ensure that acceptable methods of hunting are used in the pursuit of game and to ensure the long-term viability of game populations. They are also in place to protect you and your ability to venture into the wild and hunt game year after year. Read the hunting brochures for the state in which you will be hunting and familiarize yourself with their hunting laws and regulations. Abide by those regulations. Remember what happened to elk populations when hunting was unregulated. Elk declined from an estimated population of 10 million animals to about 100,000 animals, a 99% reduction. It is important that every hunter do his/her part to make sure nothing like that ever happens again.

Don't cheat when you hunt. Don't engage in outright illegal activity. If you observe illegal hunting, call the Fish & Game department's toll free number (in the State's hunting brochure) to report it. Be sure to have facts to report such as who, what, when and where. Don't engage in practices like "party hunting" where everyone in an elk camp continues to hunt until every tag in camp is filled. First, this practice is in violation of game laws almost everywhere and secondly, it is blatantly unethical. It is also damaging to game populations because more animals can be taken than would otherwise have been taken. If you engage in this practice, think about it as you read the following paragraphs about what fair chase means and how hunting success is not a guaranteed outcome. Party hunting does not square with fair chase. Instead of being an unprincipled hunter, hunt with honor and integrity.

One of the key aspects of fair chase is keeping the playing field of hunting on as level a plane as possible, so that the pursuer does not have undue or unfair advantage over the pursued. This means that the animal has a decent chance to win the contest with the hunter, escape, and be pursued again another day. In other words, hunter success is not guaranteed. Any practice where the hunting outcome is certain, i.e., where the hunter will always be successful, is not fair chase. It is not hunting, it is only shooting.

The finest treatise I have ever read about fair chase is the book titled *Beyond Fair Chase, The Ethics and Traditions of Hunting*, by Jim Posewitz. Jim Posewitz was a career wildlife biologist with the Montana Fish & Game Department (now called the Montana Department of Fish, Wildlife & Parks). After serving thirty-two years with the Department of Fish, Wildlife and Parks, he founded Orion – The Hunters Institute, a non-profit organization that works to promote ethical and responsible hunting. He had a long and distinguished career and is well recognized as one of the brightest beacons of ethical hunting.

Beyond Fair Chase includes a number of stories about hunting situations to help explain and illustrate key points of fair chase. One of my favorites is the story titled *A Story of a Lost Bull*. This is a story about a bowhunter who shoots at a nice bull and gets a solid hit. The bull runs off though, and despite many hours of effort searching, the hunter cannot find him. He eschewed any further hunting and continued to search for the bull, every day, even though he knew full well the bull was dead and the meat was spoiled. On the thirtieth day of searching, he found the remains of the bull, in a dense alder thicket, a place he passed by just yards away many times during his search over the previous weeks. The hunter dug into his pocket, pulled out his license tag, filled it out and attached it to the bull. His hunt was over.

That story has always struck me as one about respect, dedication, commitment and honor. I have always been impressed by it. To me, it represents many of the finest qualities that embody fair chase. This is the kind of person Fred and I would be proud to have as a hunting partner and a member of our elk camp.

Unfortunately, not everyone practices fair chase when they hunt. One of the absolute most egregious examples of the antithesis of fair chase hunting are the game farms where people (you can't call them hunters) shoot animals in fenced in areas (aka "Nine Foot

Fence Hunts"). These animals don't even have it as good as many cattle, as they are not free ranging. They are basically farm raised. People come and pay to shoot them.

There is no hunting involved in this charade. I'm sure when a group of guys show up, there is a lot of tough guy talk and bravado about who will shoot the biggest bull or buck. I'm also sure there is a bit of dress-up involved in that people will show up in their camo clothing, pretending, I suppose, they need it behind the fence. Then they get driven out into the enclosure in an ATV type vehicle, pick out a bull (or perhaps a buck if they are shooting a deer), aim and shoot. Wow! What an experience! How exciting! What a sense of accomplishment. Then it's back to the main house to knock back a beer or two or perhaps a shot or two of a single malt. Dress out the animal? Skin him out? Any packing? Are you kidding? Someone else handles all that. No need to get even a drop of blood on your hands. Some places will even video the entire experience so you can relive all that excitement of taking that farm raised trophy again and again in the comfort of your living room.

Please, this is not hunting. It's a joke to call this hunting. This is no different than going out in a farmer's field and shooting a cow. Anyone who represents or thinks this type of experience is hunting is seriously delusional. This type of experience is the exact opposite of fair chase hunting. It is a shallow, hollow experience, devoid of any sense of accomplishment and pride. There is no sense of having earned anything with this type of experience. All it is is shooting a farm raised animal.

I once worked with a guy whose idea of hunting was to go down to a very large ranch located in southern Colorado every October. This ranch was heavily populated with elk. It is a very pricey proposition, a pay-to-hunt type of place that probably cost him $10,000 or more (I never asked) each year. There is no walking or hiking involved. The method of "hunting" is to be driven around the ranch in a pickup, searching for a bull that you would be satisfied shooting.

One time, after he returned from one of his hunting trips, he showed me photos of the huge bull he had taken. He mentioned that he had had to spend almost two full days being driven around before he finally found the right bull. During that time, he had evaluated twenty-two different bulls, before finally deciding to shoot number twenty-three. No dressing out, skinning or (God forbid) packing involved here either. There are ranch hands to deal with all of that.

To me, this is not a fair chase hunt. Granted, the elk are free ranging, they are not captive like on the game farm. However, this is really nothing more than a shopping trip, like going to the mall to find a pair of shoes or a shirt. This guy doesn't even eat the meat, he gives it away. The whole objective of this exercise seems to be to collect a larger set of antlers than the previous year. Scoring the antlers is a big deal to him. There is no uncertainty about the outcome here, there is no challenge with this and no effort has been expended in the pursuit of the elk. The "hunter" is nothing more than a shooter. He knows full well that he will not leave without a nice bull.

This is another empty hunting experience. It is the type of experience that lacks substance, that is hollow. Nothing has been earned here. It's hard to have any sense of accomplishment when nothing has been earned.

When I first started hunting, back in the early 1970's, no-one scored their antlers unless they were truly anomalous and Boone & Crocket record book quality. Antler scoring is something that seems to have seeped into the hunting scene over the past twenty years or so. Now, I frequently hear other hunters boast about what their buck or bull scored. It seems that hunting for them has morphed into a contest with other hunters. I feel that the obsession among many hunters with antler scores has corrupted and degraded the hunting experience. At its essence, hunting is not a contest between hunters to see who can shoot the biggest buck or bull. It seems that the true meaning of hunting, the part about it being a balanced contest between the hunter and the game being pursued and enjoying the outdoors, is lost on many of these people.

I view hunting through a holistic lens. For me, there are many aspects of hunting that do not involve shooting an animal. I enjoy watching the sun's rays inch down the trunks of aspen trees near my tree stand as the sun rises in the east at daybreak. I enjoy watching pine martens scurry around in the pine and spruce trees near my afternoon stand. I get a thrill out of watching a chunky black bear walk by thirty yards away, unaware of my presence. I enjoy watching a magnificent, grizzled old mule deer buck wander slowly past my tree stand, noting how careful and cautious he is. I enjoy listening to the ravens call back and forth to each other as they fly above me. I doubt my former coworker has many of these experiences from the cab of the pickup while being driven around looking for that $10,000 bull.

I have been exceedingly fortunate to have taken many fine bulls, a couple of them truly exceptional. I have also been very fortunate to have taken many fine whitetail bucks in northwest Montana over the years, a number of them exceptional too. I never scored a single set of antlers. I never will. I consider every animal I shoot to be a gift from the hunting gods and a gift from nature. It makes no difference whether it is a spike bull or a huge six-point bull. Antler score has nothing to do with it.

My hunting philosophy has always been to only shoot an animal if I intend to consume it. I take no pleasure in killing any animal, least of all beautiful big game species. I also take only as much game as I actually need. Many times, I have hunted elk with both a bull tag and a cow tag in my pocket and have had the opportunity to take two elk. I have never done this though, as the meat from one animal is enough to last me an entire year. To me, there is something excessive and abusive about taking more game than you need. The hunting gods do not look favorably on those who are greedy and unprincipled.

In some parts of the country, feeders are used routinely for hunting. This type of activity (it's not hunting either) has never appealed to me. I worked in the oil and gas industry for many years and had many clients and business relationships through-out Texas and other oil and gas producing states. I liked and respected many of these people, both personally and profession-ally. Almost every year, I would receive an invitation to go down and go "deer hunting" on one ranch or lease or another. I always found a courteous and respectful way to decline. Shooting a deer, habituated to appearing just before a feeder showered the area with corn or deer pellets, has no appeal to me.

Fair chase? Nope. Challenging? Not much challenge here. Any sense of accomplishment? No. Is this hunting? No, it is just shooting. Why not just call it what it is?

I have similar problems with the practice of baiting. I remem-ber when I was dealing with an oil and gas company located in northern Michigan. One fall day I was driving from Traverse City along rural, two lane roads to the company's office about an hour's drive east. As I drove, I kept passing signs advertising corn or sugar beets for sale, sometimes with bushel baskets of the corn or beets next to them.

When I met with the CFO of the company, I asked about all the signs and baskets of corn and beets along the roads. He told me they were bait for the upcoming deer season which started a couple of weeks later. I could not believe it, "People here hunt over bait?", I asked him. He said "Of course." I asked if that was how he hunted, and he said "Sure." He explained that he didn't have the time to sit out in the woods for hours or days, waiting for a deer to show up. With bait, he almost always shot a deer the first morning.

I also know people who "hunt" bear over bait. This is really no different than hunting deer over the feeder, the pile of corn or beets or a salt lick. Call this what it really is, it's shooting. It is most definitely not hunting.

There is no fair chase in any of these activities. There is little or no uncertainty about the outcome. There is no level playing field between hunter and the quarry. The odds are all stacked in the shooter's favor. I don't think of these types of activities as hunting. They are aberrations, ways to cheat, really, by putting in little or no effort in the pursuit of game.

If you engage in these types of activities, I urge you to take two or three steps up the ethics ladder and reject this type of non-hunting. Embrace and practice fair chase in the hunting you do. Hunt with honor and integrity. Strive to become the type of person the bowhunter is in the *A Story of a Lost Bull*. You will be a better person and a better hunter for it.

CHAPTER 6

FIREARMS/HUNTING SAFETY

I end with this chapter because there is no single aspect of hunting that is more important than safe gun handling. Every year, I read or hear about "hunting accidents," where hunters are injured, sometimes killed. These are not really accidents at all, rather they are cases of carelessness and negligence.

There are a number of reasons for hunting related firearms injuries. The main reason is that people do not practice safe firearms handling.

I have been privileged to have been associated for twenty years with the finest Sheriff's Department in Colorado, the Jefferson County Sheriff Office, as a Reserve Deputy Sheriff. I have received rigorous firearms training from a cadre of outstanding firearms instructors. One of the things that is drilled into every Deputy, from the time they first attend the Department's firearms training program and continuing through their tenure with the Department, are the four basic firearms safety rules.

They are:

1. All weapons must be treated as if they are always loaded.

2. Never let the muzzle of a weapon point at anything you are not willing to destroy.

3. Keep your finger off the trigger and out of the trigger guard until your sights are on the target and you are ready to shoot.

4. Always be certain of your target and beyond.

One additional firearms safety rule that I have, is what I refer to as "action open." Whenever you hand a firearm to someone else to take a look at it, hold it for you or for any other purpose, you should always open the action before passing it to the other person. Opening the action serves two main purposes. First, it confirms that the firearm is unloaded and second, the firearm cannot fire if the action is open (aka "out of battery").

At an early age, someone in my life, I can't remember who, ingrained this practice into me and I have zealously practiced it ever since. I consider it to be a cornerstone of safe firearms handling and I use it as an indicator of whether another person possesses similar safe firearms handling habits. If someone, for example, hands me their firearm and they don't open the action, it is an immediate red flag to me that they may lack safe firearms handling habits or be casual about handling firearms safely. This is such an ingrained habit with me that I do it even when I am in a gun store. If the person behind the counter hands me a gun to take a look at, I automatically open the action when I hand it back to them, without even thinking about it.

I never pass a loaded handgun or rifle to anyone unless I open the action first. Even with the safety on, there is a risk that the firearm might be dropped or that the safety may be pushed off while it is being passed from one person to another, resulting in a possible discharge. With the action open and the firearm out of battery, there is absolutely no chance that it might fire while handling it. Just having the safety on is not enough. The safety on a firearm is nothing more than a mechanical device. They can and do fail (more on this below). While handing firearms to others, loaded or not loaded, make opening the action a habit.

One time, I was buying a Smith & Wesson Model 65 revolver from a guy with an FFL who operated his business from his home. I had ordered the gun from him and when it arrived, he called me and I headed over to his home to fill out the requisite FFL forms, pay him and pick up the revolver. I was sitting across from him at his kitchen table while he filled out some of the forms. He offered to show me his small, .25 caliber "carry" semi-auto pistol while he was doing this. He pulled the pistol from his belt holster, removed the magazine and slid the gun across the table to me. The first thing I noticed about this was that he slid the gun over with the muzzle pointed at me. I gingerly picked up the pistol, pointed it toward the floor and pulled the slide back to make sure the chamber was empty. A live round popped right out. He seemed surprised and laughed it off, saying he did not realize it was loaded (infamous last words ...). It was a good thing that his finger was not on the trigger when he passed the gun over to me.

In my view, this was really poor firearms handling, and this is with a person who is in the business of selling guns! The experience made quite an impression on me, showing me exactly how injuries, due to careless and negligent firearms handling, happen.

Most firearms injuries result from people failing to follow the basic firearms rules listed above (plus my own "action open" rule). When hunters get together in a hunting camp, they often come from all walks of life. Some hunters are avid shooters who shoot at various times throughout the year. They may hunt upland birds or waterfowl, maybe they hunt deer as well as elk, or they may belong to a gun club and shoot every month or so. They are usually very familiar with both their firearms and with firearms safety. Other hunters only go out once a year, to get away from their day to day life for a spell and get together with friends at elk camp. They may not be all that familiar with how their rifle operates. They pull their rifle case out at home, which hasn't been open since putting the rifle away the previous season and head off to go hunting. I have heard stories of people casing their rifles when they pack up to leave their elk camp, having forgotten to unload them. Then, they don't realize their rifle is still loaded when they get home and either uncase the loaded rifle to clean it or put it away loaded. A lot of really bad things can happen when you have forgotten to unload your rifle (or any firearm). I read and hear from time to time about an "accidental discharge", a situation when someone discharges a firearm unintentionally. There is really no such thing as an "accidental" discharge. There are only negligent discharges and bad things often happen when there are negligent discharges. For these reasons, as well as many others, it is imperative that strict firearms safety protocols always be followed. The consequences of not doing so can be very tragic.

One of the worst incidents I ever heard about concerning poor firearms handling occurred in Montana. A grandfather took his granddaughter out for a day of deer hunting. They parked at their destination and were preparing to head into the woods. As reconstructed by investigating game wardens later, the grandfather was standing in the open doorway on the driver's side of his pickup and his granddaughter was standing in the open doorway on the passenger side. Somehow, the grandfather discharged his rifle and the bullet passed through the cab of the pickup, hitting and killing the granddaughter on the other side. When the two hunters did not return home later that day, game wardens were contacted to search for them. They found the pickup doors still wide open, the granddaughter dead from a wound in the chest and the grandfather sitting against a nearby tree, dead from a self-inflicted wound to the head.

This is a horrible, sad story. It is also a case of firearms carelessness and negligence. The grandfather should never have allowed the muzzle of his rifle to point in the direction of his granddaughter and he should not have had his finger on the trigger.

Most, but not all, firearms incidents when hunting are caused by human carelessness or negligence. I have a good friend named G. T. Mango, known affectionately as "Magnum" due to his affinity for rifle calibers of that type. Magnum is an avid and experienced big game hunter. He has hunted elk in Montana, mule deer in Colorado, black bear in British Columbia, caribou in the Yukon and whitetail deer with me several times in northwest Montana.

One year he was hunting for coastal grizzlies on Kodiak Island in Alaska. One morning, he and his guide were in the large wall tent pitched on the edge of the beach, which served as their camp, preparing to head out for the day's hunting. Magnum was in the process of loading his fine Weatherby .340 magnum rifle. With the guide standing right next to him watching him load, Magnum worked the bolt to chamber a round. As he did so, the rifle fired, blowing a large hole in the wall of the tent. Magnum's hand was nowhere near the trigger. The rifle's action was defective. Fortunately, Magnum's firearms handling skills are excellent and the muzzle of the rifle was pointed in a safe direction, away from the guide. His strong firearms safety protocols avoided a potential disaster.

When Magnum returned home, he sent the rifle back to Weatherby, with a letter describing what had happened. Weatherby never acknowledged that there was any problem with the rifle, but they did fix it. Remington has had a similar problem with their Model 700 rifles for many years. The X-Mark Pro trigger, introduced in 2006 as a "fix" for trigger problems on earlier versions of the rifles, was no improvement. Some of the 700's with the X-Mark Pro trigger would fire spontaneously when the safety was pushed off. This is a prime example of why muzzle safety is so important ("Never let the muzzle of a weapon point at anything you are not willing to destroy".)

And then, there is my own story. In November 2013, I was walking on my family's property in northwest Montana, doing some scouting prior to the arrival of some friends for a week of whitetail deer hunting. As I was walking along a logging road on my way back to my cabins on the property, I heard a loud gunshot from down the hill, below me. Instantly my right leg did not feel right. It felt very heavy and there was a large spray of blood on the snow next to me. I had just been shot. Most of my right femur and my femoral artery had been completely blown away.

Fortunately for me and thanks to some trauma training I had received at the Jefferson County Sheriff Department, I had a tourniquet with me. It saved my life. *

The person who fired the shot was a local guy, trespassing on the property, who someway, somehow mistook me for a deer. To this day, years later, I still cannot figure out how someone can look through a telescopic sight, see the image of a person, think that it looks like a deer and squeeze the trigger. I just don't get it and I never will.

The reason I relate this incident is to show that bad things can, and do happen when hunting due to poor (often unbelievably poor) firearms handling. Other than a mechanical defect issue like the one on G. T. Mango's Weatherby or the Remington rifles, almost all hunting related firearms incidents are due to human error, i.e., carelessness and/or negligence.

You must observe absolute firearms safety protocols when you are in camp and when you are hunting. There is no room for anything less. Many firearms incidents occur around vehicles when hunters are loading or unloading their firearms (like the

*A full account of this incident is outside the scope of this book. If it is something you would be interested in learning more about, please E-Mail me at jaclevelandcolo@gmail.com and I will forward you a copy of my write up on the experience.

grandfather/granddaughter story above), exercising poor muzzle discipline or otherwise being careless or negligent in handling their firearms. Be particularly careful around vehicles. A good habit is to unload your firearm before you get to the vehicle rather than doing it at the vehicle. Do not tolerate any foolish horseplay or careless practices with firearms while in camp. Be careful with alcohol consumption in camp, as firearms and alcohol are a toxic combination. If someone in your hunting group is lax or otherwise careless about their firearms handling, suggest that they be more careful (or give them a copy of this chapter to read). You could also post a list of the four firearms safety rules in your camp. If necessary, appoint someone as a sort of Safety Officer to ensure that everyone observes a uniform level of firearms safety. Observe the four basic firearms safety rules listed above and get in the habit of handling firearms with the action open. Always remember that there is nothing more important when hunting than being safe with firearms.

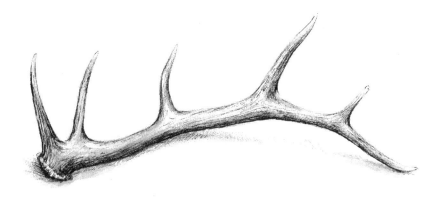

CHAPTER 7

FINAL POINTS

These are the main "Take Away" points from this book:

1. Get serious about controlling your scent

2. Glass ahead

3. The nose knows and so do the eyes – be careful with movement

4. Hunt with your rifle in your hands, not on your shoulder

5. Only shoot if you have a shot

6. Your first shot is your best shot

7. Shot placement is the most important thing – not bore size

8. Prepare – get in shape

9. Always follow up your shot – never assume you missed

10. Be an ethical and lawful hunter

11. Make Fair Chase your hunting credo

12. Firearms safety is paramount – live by the four rules of firearms safety

13. Action Open

14. Never shoot the lead cow

15. Remember, every animal taken is a gift

ABOUT
THE AUTHOR

John A. Cleveland is a lifelong outdoorsman. He first started hunting in the late 1960's, at age sixteen, for whitetail deer. He bagged his first buck the following year. He has hunted deer, upland birds, waterfowl ever since and began hunting elk in Montana in the mid-1970's. When he moved to Colorado in 1978, he started hunting elk in earnest. This book is the story of his steep learning curve and the many lessons learned over a forty-year period of elk hunting. He resides in Littleton, CO on a small ranch with his wife, dogs and horses.

RESOURCES

Jack Ballard, *Where To Hunt Elk in Montana*, Montana Outdoors, September-October 2017

Jim Posewitz, *Beyond Fair Chase, The Ethics and Traditions of Hunting*, Falcon Guides

Made in the USA
Coppell, TX
04 October 2024

38202119R00088